Contents

PREFACE

If you've already followed a BTEC First programme, you will know that this is an exciting way to study; if you are fresh from GCSEs you will find that from now on you will be in charge of your own learning. This guide has been written specially for you, to help get you started and then succeed on your BTEC National course.

The **Introduction** concentrates on making sure you have all the right facts about your course at your fingertips. Also, it guides you through the important skills you need to develop if you want to do well including:

- managing your time
- researching information
- preparing a presentation.

Keep this by your side throughout your course and dip into it whenever you need to.

The **Activities** give you tasks to do on your own, in a small group or as a class. They will help you internalise your learning and then prepare for assessment by practising your skills and showing you how much you know. These activities are not for assessment.

The sample **Assessed Assignments** show you what other students have done to gain Pass, Merit or Distinction. By seeing what past students have done, you should be able to improve your own grade.

Your BTEC National will cover six, twelve or eighteen units depending on whether you are doing an Award, Certificate or Diploma. In this guide the activities cover sections from Unit 1 – Exploring Business Activity, Unit 2 – Investigating Business Resources, Unit 3 – Introduction to Marketing and Unit 4 – Effective People, Communication and Information. These units underpin your study of Business.

Because the guide covers only four units, it is essential that you do all the other work your tutors set you. You will have to research information in textbooks, in the library and on the Internet. You should have the opportunity to visit local organisations and welcome visiting speakers to your institution. This is a great way to find out more about your chosen vocational area – the type of jobs that are available and what the work is really like.

This Guide is a taster, an introduction to your BTEC National. Use it as such and make the most of the rich learning environment that your tutors will provide for you. Your BTEC National will give you an excellent base for further study, a broad understanding of business and the knowledge you need to succeed in the world of work. Remember, thousands of students have achieved a BTEC National and are now studying for a degree or at work, building a successful career.

BTEC National
Business

A PEARSON COMPANY

BTEC National Study Guide: Business

Published by:
Edexcel Limited
One90 High Holborn
London WC1V 7BH
www.edexcel.org.uk

Distributed by:
Pearson Education Limited
Edinburgh Gate
Harlow
Essex CM20 2JE

First published 2007
Second impression 2008

ISBN: 978-1-84690-215-4

Project managed and typeset by Hart McLeod, Cambridge
Printed in Great Britain by Henry Ling Limited, at the Dorset Press, Dorchester, DT1 1HD

Cover image ©Jon Arnold Images/Alamy

The publisher's policy is to use paper manufactured from sustainable forests.

All reasonable efforts have been made to trace and contact original copyright owners.

This material offers high quality support for the delivery of Edexcel qualifications.
This does not mean that it is essential to achieve any Edexcel qualification, nor does it mean that this is the only suitable material available to support any Edexcel qualification. No Edexcel-published material will be used verbatim in setting any Edexcel assessment and any resource lists produced by Edexcel shall include this and other appropriate texts.

Acknowledgements

We are grateful to the following for permission to reproduce copyright material:

p.99 Guardian News & Media Ltd for an extract adapted from "From fast food to health food: pizza gets a makeover" by Ian Sample published in *The Guardian* 27th March 2007 copyright © The Guardian 2007; p.104 The Guide Dogs for the Blind Association for the use of their mission statement and vision copyright © www.gdba.org.uk 2007; and p.109 Ryanair for the use of their mission statement and goals copyright © www.ryanair.com 2007.

Photographs

p.41 ©Mark Baigent/Alamy; p.44 ©Justin Sullivan/Getty Images; p.47 ©Keith Shuttlewood/Alamy; p.48 ©Ian Hay/London Aerial Photo Library/Alamy; p.49 ©Paul Heinrich/Alamy; p.56 ©Stephen Hird/Reuters/Corbis; p.62 ©Jack Hollingsworth/Brand X/Corbis; p.63 ©Roger Bamber/Alamy; p.64 ©Kevin Cooley/Stone +/Getty Images; p.67 ©Daniel Berehulak/Getty Images; p.69 ©Skyscan Photolibrary/Alamy; p.79 ©Ian Francis/Alamy; p.81 Rob Barker; p.82 ©Erik Rank/Photonica/Getty Images; p.84 ©Cone 6 Productions/Brand X/Corbis; p.93 Courtesy of Apple; p.97 ©image100/Alamy, p.99 ©Paul Poplis/StockFood Creative/Getty Images

INTRODUCTION

SEVEN STEPS TO SUCCESS ON YOUR BTEC NATIONAL

You have received this guide because you have decided to do a BTEC National qualification. You may even have started your course. At this stage you should feel good about your decision. BTEC Nationals have many benefits – they are well-known and respected qualifications, they provide excellent preparation for future work or help you to get into university if that is your aim. If you are already at work then gaining a BTEC National will increase your value to your employer and help to prepare you for promotion.

Despite all these benefits though, you may be rather apprehensive about your ability to cope. Or you may be wildly enthusiastic about the whole course! More probably, you are somewhere between the two – perhaps quietly confident most of the time but sometimes worried that you may get out of your depth as the course progresses. You may be certain you made the right choice or still have days when your decision worries you. You may understand exactly what the course entails and what you have to do – or still feel rather bewildered, given all the new stuff you have to get your head around.

Your tutors will use the induction sessions at the start of your course to explain the important information they want you to know. At the time, though, it can be difficult to remember everything. This is especially true if you have just left school and are now studying in a new environment, among a group of people you have only just met. It is often only later that you think of useful questions to ask. Sometimes, misunderstandings or difficulties may only surface weeks or months into a course – and may continue for some time unless they are quickly resolved.

This student guide has been written to help to minimise these difficulties, so that you get the most out of your BTEC National course from day one. You can read through it at your own pace. You can look back at it whenever you have a problem or query.

This Introduction concentrates on making sure you have all the right facts about your course at your fingertips. This includes a **Glossary** (on page 32) which explains the specialist terms you may hear or read – including words and phrases highlighted in bold type in this Introduction.

The Introduction also guides you through the important skills you need to develop if you want to do well – such as managing your time, researching information and preparing a presentation; as well as reminding you about the key skills you will need to do justice to your work, such as good written and verbal communications.

Make sure you have all the right facts

5

- Use the PlusPoint boxes in each section to help you to stay focused on the essentials.

- Use the Action Point boxes to check out things you need to know or do right now.

- Refer to the Glossary (on page 32) if you need to check the meaning of any of the specialist terms you may hear or read.

Remember, thousands of students have achieved BTEC National Diplomas and are now studying for a degree or at work, building a successful career. Many were nervous and unsure of themselves at the outset – and very few experienced absolutely no setbacks during the course. What they did have, though, was a belief in their own ability to do well if they concentrated on getting things right one step at a time. This Introduction enables you to do exactly the same!

STEP ONE

UNDERSTAND YOUR COURSE AND HOW IT WORKS

What is a BTEC qualification and what does it involve? What will you be expected to do on the course? What can you do afterwards? How does this National differ from 'A' levels or a BTEC First qualification?

All these are common questions – but not all prospective students ask them! Did you? And, if so, did you really listen to the answers? And can you remember them now?

If you have already completed a BTEC First course then you may know some of the answers – although you may not appreciate some of the differences between that course and your new one.

Let's start by checking out the basics.

- All BTEC National qualifications are **vocational** or **work-related**. This doesn't mean that they give you all the skills that you need to do a job. It does mean that you gain the specific knowledge and understanding relevant to your chosen subject or area of work. This means that when you start in a job you will learn how to do the work more quickly and should progress further. If you are already employed, it means you become more valuable to your employer. You can choose to study a BTEC National in a wide range of vocational areas, such as Business, Health and Social Care, IT, Performing Arts and many others.

- There are three types of BTEC National qualification and each has a different number of units.

  - The BTEC National Award usually has 6 units and takes 360 **guided learning hours (GLH)** to complete. It is often offered as a part-time or short course but you may be one of the many students doing an Award alongside A-levels as a full-time course. An Award is equivalent to one 'A' level.

  - The BTEC National Certificate usually has 12 units and takes 720 GLH to complete. You may be able to study for the Certificate on a part-time or full-time course. It is equivalent to two 'A' levels.

– The BTEC National Diploma usually has 18 units and takes 1080 GLH to complete. It is normally offered as a two-year full-time course. It is equivalent to three 'A' levels.

These qualifications are often described as **nested**. This means that they fit inside each other (rather like Russian dolls!) because the same units are common to them all. This means that if you want to progress from one to another you can do so easily by simply completing more units.

- Every BTEC National qualification has a set number of **core units**. These are the compulsory units every student must complete. The number of core units you will do on your course depends upon the vocational area you are studying.

- All BTEC National qualifications also have a range of **specialist units** from which you may be able to make a choice. These enable you to study particular areas in more depth.

- Some BTEC National qualifications have **specialist core units**. These are mandatory units you will have to complete if you want to follow a particular pathway in certain vocational areas. Engineering is an example of a qualification with the overarching title, Engineering, which has a set of core units that all students must complete. Then, depending what type of engineering a student wants to follow, there are more specialist core units that must be studied.

- On all BTEC courses you are expected to be in charge of your own learning. If you have completed a BTEC First, you will already have been introduced to this idea, but you can expect the situation to be rather different now that you are working at BTEC National level. Students on a BTEC First course will be expected to need more guidance whilst they develop their skills and find their feet. In some cases, this might last quite some time. On a BTEC National course you will be expected to take more responsibility for yourself and your own learning almost from the outset. You will quickly be expected to start thinking for yourself. This means planning what to do and carrying out a task without needing constant reminders. This doesn't mean that your tutor won't give you help and guidance when you need it. It does mean, though, that you need to be 'self-starting' and to be able to use your own initiative. You also need to be able to assess your own performance and make improvements when necessary. If you enjoy having the freedom to make your own decisions and work at your own pace then you will welcome this type of learning with open arms. However, there are dangers! If you are a procrastinator (look up this word if you don't know what it means!) then it's quite likely you will quickly get in a muddle. In this case read Step 3 – Use your time wisely – very carefully indeed!

- The way you are assessed and graded on a BTEC course is different from an 'A' level course, although you will still obtain UCAS points which you need if you want to go to university. You can read about this in the next section.

PLUSPOINTS

+ You can usually choose to study part-time or full-time for your BTEC National and do an Award, Certificate or Diploma and progress easily from one to the other.

+ You will study both core units and specialist units on your course.

+ When you have completed your BTEC course you can get a job (or **apprenticeship**), use your qualification to develop your career and/or continue your studies to degree level.

+ You are responsible for your own learning on a BTEC course. This prepares you for life at work or at university when you will be expected to be self-starting and to use your own initiative.

ACTION POINTS

✓ Check you know whether you are studying for an Award, Certificate or Diploma and find out the number of units you will be studying for your BTEC National qualification.

✓ Find out which are core and which are specialist units, and which specialist units are offered at your school or college.

✓ Check out the length of your course and when you will be studying each unit.

✓ Explore the Edexcel website at www.edexcel.org.uk. Your first task is to find what's available for your particular BTEC National qualification. Start by finding National qualifications, then look for your vocational area and check you are looking at the 2007 schemes. Then find the specification for your course. Don't print this out – it is far too long. You could, of course, save it if you want to refer to it regularly or you could just look through it for interest and then bookmark the pages relating to your qualification for future reference.

✓ Score yourself out of 5 (where 0 is awful and 5 is excellent) on each of the following to see how much improvement is needed for you to become responsible for your own learning!

Being punctual; organisational ability; tidiness; working accurately; finding and correcting own mistakes; solving problems; accepting responsibility; working with details; planning how to do a job; using own initiative; thinking up new ideas; meeting deadlines.

✓ Draw up your own action plan to improve any areas where you are weak. Talk this through at your next individual **tutorial**.

STEP TWO

UNDERSTAND HOW YOU ARE ASSESSED AND GRADED – AND USE THIS KNOWLEDGE TO YOUR ADVANTAGE!

If you already have a BTEC First qualification, you may think that you don't need to read this section because you assume that BTEC National is simply more of the same. Whilst there are some broad similarities, you will now be working at an entirely different level and the grades you get for your work could be absolutely crucial to your future plans.

Equally, if you have opted for BTEC National rather than 'A' level because you thought you would have less work (or writing) to do then you need to read this section very carefully. Indeed, if you chose your BTEC National because you thought it would guarantee you an easy life, you are likely to get quite a shock when reality hits home!

It is true that, unlike 'A' levels, there are no exams on a BTEC course. However, to do well you need to understand the importance of your assignments, how these are graded and how these convert into unit points and UCAS points. This is the focus of this section.

Your assignments

On a BTEC National course your learning is assessed by means of **assignments** set by your tutors and given to you to complete throughout your course.

■ Your tutors will use a variety of **assessment methods**, such as case studies, projects, presentations and shows to obtain evidence of your skills and knowledge to date. You may also be given work-based or **time-constrained** assignments – where your performance might be observed and assessed. It will depend very much on the vocational area you are studying (see also page 16).

■ Important skills you will need to learn are how to research information (see page 25) and how to use your time effectively, particularly if you have to cope with several assignments at the same time (see page 12). You may also be expected to work cooperatively as a member of a team to complete some parts of your assignments – especially if you are doing a subject like Performing Arts – or to prepare a presentation (see page 26).

■ All your assignments are based on **learning outcomes** set by Edexcel. These are listed for each unit in your course specification. You have to meet *all* the learning outcomes to pass the unit.

Your grades

On a BTEC National course, assignments that meet the learning outcomes are graded as Pass, Merit or Distinction.

■ The difference between these grades has very little to do with how much you write! Edexcel sets out the **grading criteria** for the different grades in a **grading grid**. This identifies the **higher-level skills** you have to demonstrate to earn a higher grade. You can find out more about this, and read examples of good (and not so good) answers to assignments at Pass, Merit and Distinction level in the assessed assignments section starting on page 101. You will also find out more about getting the best grade you can in Step 5 – Understand your assessment – on page 16.

■ Your grades for all your assignments earn you **unit points**. The number of points you get for each unit is added together and your total score determines your final grade(s) for the qualification – again either Pass, Merit or Distinction. You get one final grade if you are taking a BTEC National Award, two if you are taking a BTEC National Certificate and three if you are taking a BTEC National Diploma.

■ Your points and overall grade(s) also convert to **UCAS points** which you will need if you want to apply to study on a degree course. As an example, if you are studying a BTEC National Diploma, and achieve three final pass grades you will achieve 120 UCAS points. If you achieve three final distinction grades the number of UCAS points you have earned goes up to 360.

■ It is important to note that you start earning both unit and UCAS points from the very first assignment you complete! This means that if you take a long time to settle into your course, or to start working productively, you could easily lose valuable points for quite some time. If you have your heart set on a particular university or degree course then this could limit your choices. Whichever way you look at it, it is silly to squander potentially good grades for an assignment and their equivalent points, just because you didn't really understand what you had to do – which is why this guide has been written to help you!

■ If you take a little time to understand how **grade boundaries** work, you can see where you need to concentrate your efforts to get the best final grade possible. Let's give a simple example. Chris and Shaheeda both want to go to university and have worked hard on their BTEC National Diploma course. Chris ends with a total score of 226 unit points which converts to 280 UCAS points. Shaheeda ends with a total score of 228 unit points – just two points more – which converts to 320 UCAS points! This is because a score of between 204 and 227 unit points gives 280 UCAS points, whereas a score of 228 – 251 points gives 320 UCAS points. Shaheeda is pleased because this increases her chances of getting a place on the degree course she wants. Chris is annoyed. He says if he had known then he would have put more effort into his last assignment to get two points more.

■ It is always tempting to spend time on work you like doing, rather than work you don't – but this can be a mistake if you have already done the best you can at an assignment and it would already earn a very good grade. Instead you should now concentrate on improving an assignment which covers an area where you know you are weak, because this will boost your overall grade(s). You will learn more about this in Step 3 – Use your time wisely.

10

PLUSPOINTS

+ Your learning is assessed in a variety of ways, such as by assignments, projects and case studies. You will need to be able to research effectively, manage your own time and work well with other people to succeed.

+ You need to demonstrate specific knowledge and skills to achieve the learning outcomes set by Edexcel. You need to demonstrate you can meet all the learning outcomes to pass a unit.

+ Higher-level skills are required for higher grades. The grading criteria for Pass, Merit and Distinction grades are set out in a grading grid for the unit.

+ The assessment grades of Pass, Merit and Distinction convert to unit points. The total number of unit points you receive during the course determines your final overall grade(s) and the UCAS points you have earned.

+ Working effectively from the beginning maximises your chances of achieving a good qualification grade. Understanding grade boundaries enables you to get the best final grade(s) possible.

ACTION POINTS

✓ Find the learning outcomes for the units you are currently studying. Your tutor may have given you these already, or you can find them in the specification for your course that you already accessed at www.edexcel.org.uk.

✓ Look at the grading grid for the units and identify the way the evidence required changes to achieve the higher grades. Don't worry if there are some words that you do not understand – these are explained in more detail on page 32 of this guide.

✓ If you are still unsure how the unit points system works, ask your tutor to explain it to you.

✓ Check out the number of UCAS points you would need for any course or university in which you are interested.

✓ Keep a record of the unit points you earn throughout your course and check regularly how this is affecting your overall grade(s), based on the grade boundaries for your qualification. Your tutor will give you this information or you can check it yourself in the specification for your course on the Edexcel website.

STEP THREE

USE YOUR TIME WISELY

Most students on a BTEC National course are trying to combine their course commitments with a number of others – such as a job (either full or part-time) and family responsibilities. In addition, they still want time to meet with friends, enjoy a social life and keep up hobbies and interests that they have.

Starting the course doesn't mean that you have to hide away for months if you want to do well. It does mean that you have to use your time wisely if you want to do well, stay sane and keep a balance in your life.

You will only do this if you make time work for you, rather than against you, by taking control. This means that you decide what you are doing, when you are doing it and work purposefully; rather than simply reacting to problems or panicking madly because you've yet another deadline staring you in the face.

Use your time wisely

This becomes even more important as your course progresses because your workload is likely to increase, particularly towards the end of a term. In the early days you may be beautifully organised and able to cope easily. Then you may find you have several tasks to complete simultaneously as well as some research to start. Then you get two assignments in the same week from different tutors – as well as having a presentation to prepare. Then another assignment is scheduled for the following week – and so on. This is not because your tutors are being deliberately difficult. Indeed, most will try to schedule your assignments to avoid such clashes. The problem, of course, is that none of your tutors can assess your abilities until you have learned something – so if several units start and end at the same time it is highly likely there will be some overlap between your assignments.

To cope when the going gets tough, without collapsing into an exhausted heap, you need to learn a few time management skills.

- **Pinpoint where your time goes at the moment** Time is like money – it's usually difficult to work out where it all went! Work out how much time you currently spend at college, at work, at home and on social activities. Check, too, how much time you waste each week – and why this happens. Are you disorganised or do you easily get distracted? Then identify commitments that are vital and those that are optional so that you know where you can find time if you need to.

- **Plan when and where to work** It is unrealistic not to expect to do quite a lot of work for your course in your own time. It is also better to work regularly, and in relatively short bursts, than to work just once or twice a week for very long stretches. In addition to deciding when to work, and for how long, you also need to think about when and where to work. If you are a lark, you will work better early in the day; if you are an owl, you will be at your best later on. Whatever time you work, you need somewhere quiet so that you can concentrate and with space for books and other resources you need. If the words 'quiet oasis' and 'your house' are totally incompatible at any time of the day or night

11

then check out the opening hours of your local and college library so that you have an escape route if you need it. If you are trying to combine studying with parental responsibilities it is sensible to factor in your children's commitments – and work around their bedtimes too! Store up favours, too, from friends and grandparents that you can call in if you get desperate for extra time when an assignment deadline is looming.

- **Schedule your commitments** Keep a diary or (even better) a wall chart and write down every appointment you make or task you are given. It is useful to use a colour code to differentiate between personal and work or course commitments. You may also want to enter assignment review dates with your tutor in one colour and final deadline dates in another. Keep your diary or chart up-to-date by adding any new dates promptly every time you receive another task or assignment or whenever you make any other arrangements. Keep checking ahead so that you always have prior warning when important dates are looming. This stops you from planning a heavy social week when you will be at your busiest at work or college and from arranging a dental appointment on the morning when you and your team are scheduled to give an important presentation!

- **Prioritise your work** This means doing the most important and urgent task first, rather than the one you like the most! Normally this will be the task or assignment with the nearest deadline. There are two exceptions. Sometimes you may need to send off for information and allow time for it to arrive. It is therefore sensible to do this first so that you are not held up later. The second is when you have to take account of other people's schedules – because you are working in a team or are arranging to interview someone, for example. In this case you will have to arrange your schedule around their needs, not just your own.

- **Set sensible timescales** Trying to do work at the last minute or in a rush is never satisfactory, so it is wise always to allocate more time than you think you will need, never less. Remember, too, to include all the stages of a complex task or assignment, such as researching the information, deciding what to use, creating a first draft, checking it and making improvements and printing it out. If you are planning to do any of your work in a central facility always allow extra time and try to start work early. If you arrive at the last minute you may find every computer and printer is fully utilised until closing time.

- **Learn self-discipline!** This means not putting things off (procrastinating!) because you don't know where to start or don't feel in the mood. Unless you are ill, you have to find some way of persuading yourself to work. One way is to bribe yourself. Make a start and promise yourself that if you work productively for 30 minutes then you deserve a small reward. After 30 minutes you may have become more engrossed and want to keep going a little longer. Otherwise at least you have made a start, so it's easier to come back and do more later. It doesn't matter whether you have research to do, an assignment to write up, a coaching session to plan, or lines to learn, you need to be self-disciplined.

- **Take regular breaks and keep your life in balance** Don't go to the opposite extreme and work for hours on end. Take regular breaks to give yourself a rest and a change of activity. You need to recharge your batteries! Similarly, don't cancel every social arrangement so that you can work 24/7. Whilst this may be occasionally necessary if you have several deadlines looming simultaneously, it should only be a last resort. If you find yourself doing this regularly then go back to the beginning of this section and see where your time–management planning is going wrong.

PLUSPOINTS

+ Being in control of your time enables you to balance your commitments according to their importance and allows you not let to anyone down – including yourself.

+ Controlling time involves knowing how you spend (and waste!) your time now, planning when best to do work, scheduling your commitments and setting sensible timescales for work to be done.

+ Knowing how to prioritise means that you will schedule work effectively according to its urgency and importance but this also requires self-discipline. You have to follow the schedule you have set for yourself!

+ Managing time and focusing on the task at hand means you will do better work and be less stressed, because you are not having to react to problems or crises. You can also find the time to include regular breaks and leisure activities in your schedule.

ACTION POINTS

✓ Find out how many assignments you can expect to receive this term and when you can expect to receive these. Enter this information into your student diary or onto a planner you can refer to regularly.

✓ Update your diary and/or planner with other commitments that you have this term – both work/college-related and social. Identify any potential clashes and decide the best action to take to solve the problem.

✓ Identify your own best time and place to work quietly and effectively.

✓ Displacement activities are things we do to put off starting a job we don't want to do – such as sending texts, watching TV, checking emails etc. Identify yours so that you know when you're doing them!

STEP FOUR

UTILISE ALL YOUR RESOURCES

Your resources are all the things that can help you to achieve your qualification. They can therefore be as wide-ranging as your favourite website and your **study buddy** (see below) who collects handouts for you if you miss a class.

Your college will provide the essential resources for your course, such as a library with a wide range of books and electronic reference sources, learning resource centre(s), the computer network and Internet access. Other basic resources you will be expected to provide yourself, such as file folders and paper. The policy on textbooks varies from one college to another, but on most courses today students are expected to buy their own. If you look after yours carefully, then you have the option to sell it on to someone else afterwards and recoup some of your money. If you scribble all over it, leave it on the floor and then tread on it, turn back pages and rapidly turn it into a dog-eared, misshapen version of its former self then you miss out on this opportunity.

Unfortunately students often squander other opportunities to utilise resources in the best way – usually because they don't think about them very much, if at all. To help, below is a list of the resources you should consider important – with a few tips on how to get the best out of them.

- **Course information** This includes your course specification, this Study Guide and all the other information relating to your BTEC National which you can find on the Edexcel website. Add to this all the information given to you at college relating to your course, including term dates, assignment dates and, of course, your timetable. This should not be 'dead' information that you glance at once and then discard or ignore. Rather it is important reference material that you need to store somewhere obvious, so that you can look at it whenever you have a query or need to clarify something quickly.

- **Course materials** In this group is your textbook (if there is one), the handouts you are given as well as print-outs and notes you make yourself. File handouts the moment you are given them and put them into an A4 folder bought for the purpose. You will need one for each unit you study. Some students prefer lever-arch files but these are more bulky so more difficult to carry around all day. Unless you have a locker at college it can be easier to keep a lever arch file at home for permanent storage of past handouts and notes for a unit and carry an A4 folder with you which contains current topic information. Filing handouts and print-outs promptly means they don't get lost. They are also less likely to get crumpled, torn or tatty becoming virtually unreadable. Unless you have a private and extensive source of income then this is even more important if you have to pay for every print-out you take in your college resource centre. If you are following a course such as Art and Design, then there will be all your art materials and the pieces you produce. You must look after these with great care.

- **Other stationery items** Having your own pens, pencils, notepad, punch, stapler and sets of dividers is essential. Nothing irritates tutors more than watching one punch circulate around a group – except, perhaps, the student who trudges into class with nothing to write on or with. Your dividers should be clearly labelled to help you store and find notes, print-outs and handouts fast. Similarly, your notes should be clearly headed and dated. If you are writing notes up from your own research then you will have to include your source. Researching information is explained in Step 6 – Sharpen your skills.

- **Equipment and facilities** These include your college library and resource centres, the college computer network and other college equipment you can use, such as laptop computers, photocopiers and presentation equipment. Much of this may be freely available; others – such as using the photocopier in the college library or the printers in a resource centre – may cost you money. Many useful resources will be electronic, such as DVDs or electronic journals and databases. At home you may have your own computer with Internet access to count as a resource. Finally, include any specialist equipment and facilities available for your particular course that you use at college or have at home.

All centralised college resources and facilities are invaluable if you know

Utilise all your resources

how to use them – but can be baffling when you don't. Your induction should have included how to use the library, resource centre(s) and computer network. You should also have been informed of the policy on using IT equipment which determines what you can and can't do when you are using college computers. If, by any chance, you missed this then go and check it out for yourself. Library and resource centre staff will be only too pleased to give you helpful advice – especially if you pick a quiet time to call in. You can also find out about the allowable ways to transfer data between your college computer and your home computer if your options are limited because of IT security.

Having a study buddy is a good idea

- **People** You are surrounded by people who are valuable resources: your tutor(s), specialist staff at college, your employer and work colleagues, your relatives and any friends who have particular skills or who work in the same area you are studying. Other members of your class are also useful resources – although they may not always seem like it! Use them, for example, to discuss topics out of class time. A good debate between a group of students can often raise and clarify issues that there may not be time to discuss fully in class. Having a study buddy is another good idea – you get/make notes for them when they are away and vice versa. That way you don't miss anything.

If you want information or help from someone, especially anyone outside your immediate circle, then remember to get the basics right! Approach them courteously, do your homework first so that you are well-prepared and remember that you are asking for assistance – not trying to get them to do the work for you! If someone has agreed to allow you to interview them as part of your research for an assignment or project then good preparations will be vital, as you will see in Step 6 – Sharpen your Skills (see page 22).

One word of warning: be wary about using information from friends or relatives who have done a similar or earlier course. First, the slant of the material they were given may be different. It may also be out-of-date. And *never* copy anyone else's written assignments. This is **plagiarism** – a deadly sin in the educational world. You can read more about this in Step 5 – Understand your assessment (see page 16).

- **You!** You have the ability to be your own best resource or your own worst enemy! The difference depends upon your work skills, your personal skills and your attitude to your course and other people. You have already seen how to use time wisely. Throughout this guide you will find out how to sharpen and improve other work and personal skills and how to get the most out of your course – but it is up to you to read it and apply your new-found knowledge! This is why attributes like a positive attitude, an enquiring mind and the ability to focus on what is important all have a major impact on your final result.

15

PLUSPOINTS

+ Resources help you to achieve your qualification. You will squander these unwittingly if you don't know what they are or how to use them properly.

+ Course information needs to be stored safely for future reference: course materials need to be filed promptly and accurately so that you can find them quickly.

+ You need your own set of key stationery items; you also need to know how to use any central facilities or resources such as the library, learning resource centres and your computer network.

+ People are often a key resource – school or college staff, work colleagues, members of your class, people who are experts in their field.

+ You can be your own best resource! Develop the skills you need to be able to work quickly and accurately and to get the most out of other people who can help you.

ACTION POINTS

✓ Under the same headings as in this section, list all the resources you need for your course and tick off those you currently have. Then decide how and when you can obtain anything vital that you lack.

✓ Check that you know how to access and use all the shared resources to which you have access at school or college.

✓ Pair up with someone on your course as a study buddy – and don't let them down!

✓ Test your own storage systems. How fast can you find notes or print-outs you made yesterday/last week/last month – and what condition are they in?

✓ Find out the IT policy at your school or college and make sure you abide by it.

STEP FIVE

UNDERSTAND YOUR ASSESSMENT

The key to doing really, really well on any BTEC National course is to understand exactly what you are expected to do in your assignments – and then to do it! It really is as simple as that. So why is it that some people go wrong?

Obviously you may worry that an assignment may be so difficult that it is beyond you. Actually this is highly unlikely to happen because all your assignments are based on topics you will have already covered thoroughly in class. Therefore, if you have attended regularly – and have clarified any queries or worries you have either in class or during your tutorials – this shouldn't happen. If you have had an unavoidable lengthy absence then you may need to review your progress with your tutor and decide how best to cope with the situation. Otherwise, you should note that the main problems with assignments are usually due to far more mundane pitfalls – such as:

✗ not reading the instructions or the assignment brief properly

✗ not understanding what you are supposed to do

✗ only doing part of the task or answering part of a question

✗ skimping the preparation, the research or the whole thing

✗ not communicating your ideas clearly

✗ guessing answers rather than researching properly

✗ padding out answers with irrelevant information

✗ leaving the work until the last minute and then doing it in a rush

✗ ignoring advice and feedback your tutor has given you.

You can avoid all of these traps by following the guidelines below so that you know exactly what you are doing, prepare well and produce your best work.

The assignment 'brief'

The word 'brief' is just another way of saying 'instructions'. Often, though, a 'brief' (despite its name!) may be rather longer. The brief sets the context for the work, defines what evidence you will need to produce and matches the grading criteria to the tasks. It will also give you a schedule for completing the tasks. For example, a brief may include details of a case study you have to read; research you have to carry out or a task you have to do, as well as questions you have to answer. Or it may give you details about a project or group presentation you have to prepare. The type of assignments you receive will depend partly upon the vocational area you are studying, but you can expect some to be in the form of written assignments. Others are likely to be more practical or project-based, especially if you are doing a very practical subject such as Art and Design, Performing Arts or Sport. You may also be assessed in the workplace. For example, this is a course requirement if you are studying Children's Care, Learning and Development.

The assignment brief may also include the **learning outcomes** to which it relates. These tell you the purpose of the assessment and the knowledge you need to demonstrate to obtain a required grade. If your brief doesn't list the learning outcomes, then you should check this information against the unit specification to see the exact knowledge you need to demonstrate.

The grade(s) you can obtain will also be stated on the assignment brief. Sometimes an assignment will focus on just one grade. Others may give you the opportunity to develop or extend your work to progress to a higher grade. This is often dependent upon submitting acceptable work at the previous grade first. You will see examples of this in the Assessed Assignment section of this Study Guide on page 101.

The brief will also tell you if you have to do part of the work as a member of a group. In this case, you must identify your own contribution. You may also be expected to take part in a **peer review**, where you all give feedback on the contribution of one another. Remember that you should do this as objectively and professionally as possible – not just praise everyone madly in the hope that they will do the same for you! In any assignment where there is a group contribution, there is virtually always an individual component, so that your individual grade can be assessed accurately.

Finally, your assignment brief should state the final deadline for handing in the work as well as any interim review dates when you can discuss your progress and ideas with your tutor. These are very important dates indeed and should be entered immediately into your diary or planner. You should schedule your work around these dates so that you have made a start by the first date. This will then enable you to note any queries or significant issues you want to discuss. Otherwise you will waste a valuable opportunity to obtain useful feedback on your progress. Remember, too, to take a notebook to any review meetings so that you can write down the guidance you are given.

Your school or college rules and regulations

Your school or college will have a number of policies and guidelines about assignments and assessment. These will deal with issues such as:

- The procedure you must follow if you have a serious personal problem so cannot meet the deadline date and need an extension.

- Any penalties for missing a deadline date without any good reason.

- The penalties for copying someone else's work (**plagiarism**). These will be severe so make sure that you never share your work (including your CDs) with anyone else and don't ask to borrow theirs.

- The procedure to follow if you are unhappy with the final grade you receive.

Even though it is unlikely that you will ever need to use any of these policies, it is sensible to know they exist, and what they say, just as a safeguard.

Understanding the question or task

There are two aspects to a question or task that need attention. The first are the *command words*, which are explained below. The second are the *presentation instructions*, so that if you are asked to produce a table or graph or report then you do exactly that – and don't write a list or an essay instead!

Command words are used to specify how a question must be answered, eg 'explain', 'describe', 'analyse', 'evaluate'. These words relate to the type of answer required. So whereas you may be asked to 'describe' something at Pass level, you will need to do more (such as 'analyse' or 'evaluate') to achieve Merit or Distinction grade.

Many students fail to get a higher grade because they do not realise the difference between these words. They simply don't know *how* to analyse or evaluate, so give an explanation instead. Just adding to a list or giving a few more details will never give you a higher grade – instead you need to change your whole approach to the answer.

The **grading grid** for each unit of your course gives you the command words, so that you can find out exactly what you have to do in each unit, to obtain a Pass, Merit and Distinction. The following charts show you what is usually required when you see a particular command word. You can use this, and the assessed assignments on pages 101–142, to see the difference between the types of answers required for each grade. (The assignments your centre gives you will be specially written to ensure you have the opportunity to achieve all the possible grades.) Remember, though, that these are just examples to guide you. The exact response will often depend upon the way a question is worded, so if you have any doubts at all check with your tutor before you start work.

There are two other important points to note:

- Sometimes the same command word may be repeated for different grades – such as 'create' or 'explain'. In this case the *complexity* or *range* of the task itself increases at the higher grades – as you will see if you read the grading grid for the unit.

- Command words can also vary depending upon your vocational area. If you are studying Performing Arts or Art and Design you will probably find several command words that an Engineer or IT Practitioner would not – and vice versa!

To obtain a Pass grade

To achieve this grade you must usually demonstrate that you understand the important facts relating to a topic and can state these clearly and concisely.

Command word	What this means
Create (or produce)	Make, invent or construct an item.
Describe	Give a clear, straightforward description that includes all the main points and links these together logically.
Define	Clearly explain what a particular term means and give an example, if appropriate, to show what you mean.
Explain . . . how/why	Set out in detail the meaning of something, with reasons. It is often helpful to give an example of what you mean. Start with the topic then give the 'how' or 'why'.
Identify	Distinguish and state the main features or basic facts relating to a topic.
Interpret	Define or explain the meaning of something.
Illustrate	Give examples to show what you mean.
List	Provide the information required in a list rather than in continuous writing.
Outline	Write a clear description that includes all the main points but avoid going into too much detail.
Plan (or devise)	Work out and explain how you would carry out a task or activity.
Select (and present) information	Identify relevant information to support the argument you are making and communicate this in an appropriate way.
State	Write a clear and full account.
Undertake	Carry out a specific activity.
Examples: **Identify** the main features on a digital camera. **Describe** your usual lifestyle. **Outline** the steps to take to carry out research for an assignment.	

To obtain a Merit grade

To obtain this grade you must prove that you can apply your knowledge in a specific way.

Command word	What this means
Analyse	Identify separate factors, say how they are related and how each one relates to the topic.
Classify	Sort your information into appropriate categories before presenting or explaining it.
Compare and contrast	Identify the main factors that apply in two or more situations and explain the similarities and differences or advantages and disadvantages.
Demonstrate	Provide several relevant examples or appropriate evidence which support the arguments you are making. In some vocational areas this may also mean giving a practical performance.
Discuss	Provide a thoughtful and logical argument to support the case you are making.
Explain (in detail)	Provide details and give reasons and/or evidence to clearly support the argument you are making.
Implement	Put into practice or operation. You may also have to interpret or justify the effect or result.
Interpret	Understand and explain an effect or result.
Justify	Give appropriate reasons to support your opinion or views and show how you arrived at these conclusions.
Relate/report	Give a full account of, with reasons.
Research	Carry out a full investigation.
Specify	Provide full details and descriptions of selected items or activities.

Examples:

Compare and contrast the performance of two different digital cameras.
Justify your usual lifestyle.
Explain in detail the steps to take to research an assignment.

To obtain a Distinction grade

To obtain this grade you must prove that you can make a reasoned judgement based on appropriate evidence.

Command word	What this means
Analyse	Identify the key factors, show how they are linked and explain the importance and relevance of each.
Assess	Give careful consideration to all the factors or events that apply and identify which are the most important and relevant with reasons for your views.
Comprehensively explain	Give a very detailed explanation that covers all the relevant points and give reasons for your views or actions.
Comment critically	Give your view after you have considered all the evidence, particularly the importance of both the relevant positive and negative aspects.
Evaluate	Review the information and then bring it together to form a conclusion. Give evidence to support each of your views or statements.
Evaluate critically	Review the information to decide the degree to which something is true, important or valuable. Then assess possible alternatives taking into account their strengths and weaknesses if they were applied instead. Then give a precise and detailed account to explain your opinion.
Summarise	Identify review the main, relevant factors and/or arguments so that these are explained in a clear and concise manner.

Examples:

Assess ten features commonly found on a digital camera.
Evaluate critically your usual lifestyle.
Analyse your own ability to carry out effective research for an assignment.

Responding positively

This is often the most important attribute of all! If you believe that assignments give you the opportunity to demonstrate what you know and how you can apply it *and* positively respond to the challenge by being determined to give it your best shot, then you will do far better than someone who is defeated before they start.

It obviously helps, too, if you are well organised and have confidence in your own abilities – which is what the next section is all about!

PLUSPOINTS

+ Many mistakes in assignments are through errors that can easily be avoided such as not reading the instructions properly or doing only part of the task that was set!

+ Always read the assignment brief very carefully indeed. Check that you understand exactly what you have to do and the learning outcomes you must demonstrate.

+ Make a note of the deadline for an assignment and any interim review dates on your planner. Schedule work around these dates so that you can make the most of reviews with your tutor.

+ Make sure you know about school or college policies relating to assessment, such as how to obtain an extension or query a final grade.

+ For every assignment, make sure you understand the command words, which tell you how to answer the question, and the presentation instructions, which say what you must produce.

+ Command words are shown in the grading grid for each unit of your qualification. Expect command words and/or the complexity of a task to be different at higher grades, because you have to demonstrate higher-level skills.

ACTION POINTS

✓ Discuss with your tutor the format (style) of assignments you are likely to receive on your course, eg assignments, projects, or practical work where you are observed.

✓ Check the format of the assignments in the Assessed Assignments section of this book. Look at the type of work students did to gain a Pass and then look at the difference in the Merit answers. Read the tutor's comments carefully and ask your own tutor if there is anything you do not understand.

✓ Check out all the policies and guidelines at your school or college that relate to assessment and make sure you understand them.

✓ Check out the grading grid for the units you are currently studying and identify the command words for each grade. Then check you understand what they mean using the explanations above. If there are any words that are not included, ask your tutor to explain the meanings and what you would be required to do.

STEP SIX

SHARPEN YOUR SKILLS

To do your best in any assignment you need a number of skills. Some of these may be vocationally specific, or professional, skills that you are learning as part of your course – such as acting or dancing if you are taking a Performing Arts course or, perhaps, football if you are following a Sports course. Others, though, are broader skills that will help you to do well in assignments no matter what subjects or topics you are studying – such as communicating clearly and cooperating with others.

Some of these skills you will have already and in some areas you may be extremely proficient. Knowing where your weaknesses lie, though, and doing something about them has many benefits. You will work more quickly, more accurately *and* have increased confidence in your own abilities. As an extra bonus, all these skills also make you more effective at work – so there really is no excuse for not giving yourself a quick skills check and then remedying any problem areas.

This section contains hints and tips to help you check out and improve each of the following areas:

- Your numeracy skills
- Keyboarding and document preparation
- Your IT skills
- Your written communication skills
- Working with others
- Researching information
- Making a presentation
- Problem solving and staying focused

Improving your numeracy skills

Some people have the idea that they can ignore numeracy because this skill isn't relevant to their vocational area – such as Art and Design or Children's Care, Learning and Development. If this is how you think then you are wrong! Numeracy is a life skill that everyone needs, so if you can't carry out basic calculations accurately then you will have problems, often when you least expect them.

Fortunately there are several things you can do to remedy this situation:

- Practise basic calculations in your head and then check them on a calculator.
- Ask your tutor if there are any essential calculations which give you difficulties.
- Use your onscreen calculator (or a spreadsheet package) to do calculations for you when you are using your computer.
- Try your hand at Sudoku puzzles – either on paper or by using a software package or online at sites such as www.websudoku.com/.
- Investigate puzzle sites and brain training software, such as http://school.discovery.com/brainboosters/ and Dr Kawashima's Brain Training by Nintendo.
- Check out online sites such as www.bbc.co.uk/skillswise/ and www.bbc.co.uk/schools/ks3bitesize/maths/number/index.shtml to improve your skills.

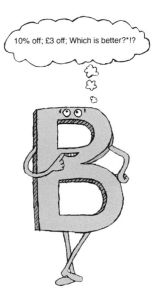

Numeracy is a life skill

Keyboarding and document preparation

- Think seriously about learning to touch type to save hours of time! Your school or college may have a workshop you can join or you can learn online such as by downloading a free program at www.sense-lang.org/typing/ or practising on sites such as www.computerlab.kids.new.net/keyboarding.htm.
- Obtain correct examples of document formats you will have to use, such as a report or summary. Your tutor may provide you with these or you can find examples in many communication textbooks.
- Proofread work you produce on a computer *carefully*. Remember that your spell checker will not pick up every mistake you make, such as a mistyped word that makes another word (eg form/from; sheer/shear)

and grammar checkers, too, are not without their problems! This means you still have to read your work through yourself. If possible, let your work go 'cold' before you do this so that you read it afresh and don't make assumptions about what you have written. Then read word by word to make sure it still makes sense and there are no silly mistakes, such as missing or duplicated words.

- Make sure your work looks professional by using an appropriate typeface and font size as well as suitable margins.
- Print out your work carefully and store it neatly, so it looks in pristine condition when you hand it in.

Your IT skills

- Check that you can use the main features of all the software packages that you will need to produce your assignments, such as Word, Excel and PowerPoint.
- Adopt a good search engine, such as Google, and learn to use it properly. Many have online tutorials such as www.googleguide.com.
- Develop your IT skills to enable you to enhance your assignments appropriately. For example, this may include learning how to import and export text and artwork from one package to another; taking digital photographs and inserting them into your work and/or creating drawings or diagrams by using appropriate software for your course.

Your written communication skills

A poor vocabulary will reduce your ability to explain yourself clearly; work peppered with spelling or punctuation errors looks unprofessional.

- Read more. This introduces you to new words and familiarises you over and over again with the correct way to spell words.
- Look up words you don't understand in a dictionary and then try to use them yourself in conversation.
- Use the Thesaurus in Word to find alternatives to words you find yourself regularly repeating, to add variety to your work.
- *Never* use words you don't understand in the hope that they sound impressive!
- Do crosswords to improve your word power and spelling.
- Resolve to master punctuation – especially apostrophes – either by using an online programme or working your way through the relevant section of a communication textbook that you like.
- Check out online sites such as www.bbc.co.uk/skillswise/ and www.bbc.co.uk/schools/gcsebitesize/english/ as well as puzzle sites with communication questions such as http://school.discovery.com/brainboosters/.

Working with others

In your private life you can choose who you want to be with and how you respond to them. At work you cannot do that – you are paid to be professional and this means working alongside a wide variety of people, some of whom you may like and some of whom you may not!

The same applies at school or college. By the time you have reached BTEC National level you will be expected to have outgrown wanting to work with your best friends on every project! You may not be very keen on everyone who is in the same team as you, but – at the very least – you can be pleasant, cooperative and helpful. In a large group this isn't normally too difficult. You may find it much harder if you have to partner someone who has very different ideas and ways of working to you.

In this case it may help if you:

- Realise that everyone is different and that your ways of working may not always be the best!
- Are prepared to listen and contribute to a discussion (positively) in equal amounts. Make sure, too, that you encourage the quiet members of the group to speak up by asking them what their views are. The ability to draw other people into the discussion is an important and valuable skill to learn.
- Write down what you have said you will do, so that you don't forget anything.
- Are prepared to do your fair share of the work.
- Discuss options and alternatives with people – don't give them orders or meekly accept instructions and then resent it afterwards.
- Don't expect other people to do what you wouldn't be prepared to do.
- Are sensitive to other people's feelings and remember that they may have personal problems or issues that affect their behaviour.
- *Always* keep your promises and never let anyone down when they are depending upon you.
- Don't flounce around or lose your temper if things get tough. Instead take a break while you cool down. Then sit down and discuss the issues that are annoying you.
- Help other people to reach a compromise when necessary, by acting as peacemaker.

Researching information

Poor researchers either cannot find what they want or find too much – and then drown in a pile of papers. If you find yourself drifting aimlessly around a library when you want information or printing out dozens of pages for no apparent purpose, then this section is for you!

- Always check *exactly* what it is you need to find and how much detail is needed. Write down a few key words to keep yourself focused.
- Discipline yourself to ignore anything that is irrelevant – from books with interesting titles to websites which sound tempting but have little to do with your topic or key words.
- Remember that you could theoretically research information forever! So at some time you have to call a halt. Learning when to do this is another skill, but you can learn this by writing out a schedule which clearly states when you have to stop looking and start sorting out your information and writing about it!

- In a library, check you know how the books are stored and what other types of media are available. If you can't find what you are looking for then ask the librarian for help. Checking the index in a book is the quickest way to find out whether it contains information related to your key words. Put it back if it doesn't or if you can't understand it. If you find three or four books and/or journals that contain what you need then that is usually enough.

- Online use a good search engine and use the summary of the search results to check out the best sites. Force yourself to check out sites beyond page one of the search results! When you enter a site investigate it carefully – use the site map if necessary. It isn't always easy to find exactly what you want. Bookmark sites you find helpful and will want to use again and only take print-outs when the information is closely related to your key words.

- Talk to people who can help you (see also Step 4 – Utilise all your resources) and prepare in advance by thinking about the best questions to ask. Always explain why you want the information and don't expect anyone to tell you anything that is confidential or sensitive – such as personal information or financial details. Always write clear notes so that you remember what you have been told, by whom and when. If you are wise you will also note down their contact details so that you can contact them again if you think of anything later. If you remember to be courteous and thank them for their help, this shouldn't be a problem.

- Store all your precious information carefully and neatly in a labelled folder so that you can find it easily. Then, when you are ready to start work, reread it and extract that which is most closely related to your key words and the task you are doing.

- Make sure you state the source of all the information you quote by including the name of the author or the web address, either in the text or as part of a bibliography at the end. Your school or college will have a help sheet which will tell you exactly how to do this.

Making a presentation

This involves several skills – which is why it is such a popular way of finding out what students can do! It will test your ability to work in a team, speak in public and use IT (normally PowerPoint) – as well as your nerves. It is therefore excellent practice for many of the tasks you will have to do when you are at work – from attending an interview to talking to an important client.

You will be less nervous if you have prepared well and have rehearsed your role beforehand. You will produce a better, more professional presentation if you take note of the following points.

- If you are working as a team, work out everyone's strengths and weaknesses and divide up the work (fairly) taking these into account. Work out, too, how long each person should speak and who would be the best as the 'leader' who introduces each person and then summarises everything at the end.

PLUSPOINTS

+ Poor numeracy skills can let you down in your assignments and at work. Work at improving these if you regularly struggle with even simple calculations.

+ Good keyboarding, document production and IT skills can save you hours of time and mean that your work is of a far more professional standard. Improve any of these areas which are letting you down.

+ Your written communication skills will be tested in many assignments. Work at improving areas of weakness, such as spelling, punctuation or vocabulary.

+ You will be expected to work cooperatively with other people both at work and during many assignments. Be sensitive to other people's feelings, not just your own, and always be prepared to do your fair share of the work and help other people when you can.

+ To research effectively you need to know exactly what you are trying to find and where to look. This means understanding how reference media is stored in your library as well as how to search online. Good organisation skills also help so that you store important information carefully and can find it later. And never forget to include your sources in a bibliography.

+ Making a presentation requires several skills and may be nerve-racking at first. You will reduce your problems if you prepare well, are not too ambitious and have several run-throughs beforehand. Remember to speak clearly and a little more slowly than normal and smile from time to time!

ACTION POINTS

✓ Test both your numeracy and literacy skills at http://www.move-on.org.uk/testyourskills.asp# to check your current level. You don't need to register on the site if you click to do the 'mini-test' instead. If either need improvement, get help at http://www.bbc.co.uk/keyskills/it/1.shtml.

✓ Do the following two tasks with a partner to jerk your brain into action!

- Each write down 36 simple calculations in a list, eg 8 x 6, 19 – 8, 14 + 6. Then exchange lists. See who can answer the most correctly in the shortest time.

- Each write down 30 short random words (no more than 8 letters), eg cave, table, happily. Exchange lists. You each have three minutes to try to remember as many words as possible. Then hand back the list and write down all those you can recall. See who can remember the most.

✓ Assess your own keyboarding, proof-reading, document production, written communication and IT skills. Then find out if your tutors agree with you!

✓ List ten traits in other people that drive you mad. Then, for each one, suggest what you could do to cope with the problem (or solve it) rather than make a fuss. Compare your ideas with other members of your group.

✓ Take a note of all feedback you receive from your tutors, especially in relation to working with other people, researching and giving presentations. In each case focus on their suggestions and ideas so that you continually improve your skills throughout the course.

■ Don't be over-ambitious. Take account of your time-scale, resources and the skills of the team. Remember that a simple, clear presentation is often more professional than an over-elaborate or complicated one where half the visual aids don't work properly!

■ If you are using PowerPoint try to avoid preparing every slide with bullet points! For variety, include some artwork and vary the designs. Remember that you should *never* just read your slides to the audience! Instead prepare notes that you can print out that will enable you to enhance and extend what the audience is reading.

27

- Your preparations should also include checking the venue and time; deciding what to wear and getting it ready; preparing, checking and printing any handouts; deciding what questions might be asked and how to answer these.

- Have several run-throughs beforehand and check your timings. Check, too, that you can be heard clearly. This means lifting up your head and 'speaking' to the back of the room a little more slowly and loudly than you normally do.

- On the day, arrive in plenty of time so that you aren't rushed or stressed. Remember that taking deep breaths helps to calm your nerves.

- Start by introducing yourself clearly and smile at the audience. If it helps, find a friendly face and pretend you are just talking to that person.

- Answer any questions honestly and don't exaggerate, guess or waffle. If you don't know the answer then say so!

- If you are giving the presentation in a team, help out someone else who is struggling with a question if you know the answer.

- Don't get annoyed or upset if you get any negative feedback afterwards. Instead take note so that you can concentrate on improving your own performance next time. And don't focus on one or two criticisms and ignore all the praise you received! Building on the good and minimising the bad is how everyone improves in life!

STEP SEVEN

MAXIMISE YOUR OPPORTUNITIES AND MANAGE YOUR PROBLEMS

Like most things in life, you may have a few ups and downs on your course – particularly if you are studying over quite a long time, such as one or two years. Sometimes everything will be marvellous – you are enjoying all the units, you are up-to-date with your work, you are finding the subjects interesting and having no problems with any of your research tasks. At other times you may struggle a little more. You may find one or two topics rather tedious, or there may be distractions or worries in your personal life that you have to cope with. You may struggle to concentrate on the work and do your best.

Rather than just suffering in silence or gritting your teeth if things go a bit awry it is sensible if you have an action plan to help you cope. Equally, rather than just accepting good opportunities for additional experiences or learning, it is also wise to plan how to make the best of these. This section will show you how to do this.

Making the most of your opportunities

The following are examples of opportunities to find out more about information relevant to your course or to try putting some of your skills into practice.

- **External visits** You may go out of college on visits to different places or organisations. These are not days off – there is a reason for making each trip. Prepare in advance by reading around relevant topics and make notes of useful information whilst you are there. Then write (or type) it up neatly as soon as you can and file it where you can find it again!

- **Visiting speakers** Again, people are asked to talk to your group for a purpose. You are likely to be asked to contribute towards questions that may be asked – which may be submitted in advance so that the speaker is clear on the topics you are studying. Think carefully about information that you would find helpful so that you can ask one or two relevant and useful questions. Take notes whilst the speaker is addressing your group, unless someone is recording the session. Be prepared to thank the speaker on behalf of your group if you are asked to do so.

- **Professional contacts** These will be the people you meet on work experience doing the real job that one day you hope to do. Make the most of meeting these people to find out about the vocational area of your choice.

- **Work experience** If you need to undertake practical work for any particular units of your BTEC National qualification, and if you are studying full-time, then your tutor will organise a work experience placement for you and talk to you about the evidence you need to obtain. You may also be issued with a special log book or diary in which to record your experiences. Before you start your placement, check that you are clear about all the details, such as the time you will start and leave, the name of your supervisor, what you should wear and what you should do if you are ill during the placement and cannot attend. Read and reread the units to which your evidence will apply and make sure you understand the grading criteria and what you need to obtain. Then make a note of appropriate headings to record your information. Try to make time to write up your notes, log book and/or diary every night, whilst your experiences are fresh in your mind.

- **In your own workplace** You may be studying your BTEC National qualification on a part-time basis and also have a full-time job in the same vocational area. Or you may be studying full-time and have a part-time job just to earn some money. In either case you should be alert to opportunities to find out more about topics that relate to your workplace, no matter how generally. For example, many BTEC courses include topics such as health and safety, teamwork, dealing with customers, IT security and communications – to name but a few. All these are topics that your employer will have had to address and finding out more about these will broaden your knowledge and help to give more depth to your assignment responses.

- **Television programmes, newspapers, Podcasts and other information sources.** No matter what vocational area you are studying, the media are likely to be an invaluable source of information. You should be alert to any news bulletins that relate to your studies as well as relevant information in more topical television programmes. For example, if you are studying Art and Design then you should make a particular effort to watch the *Culture Show* as well as programmes on artists, exhibitions or other topics of interest. Business students should find inspiration by watching *Dragons Den*, *The Apprentice* and the *Money Programme* and Travel and Tourism students should watch holiday, travel and adventure programmes. If you are studying Media, Music and Performing Arts then you are spoiled for choice! Whatever your vocational choice, there will be television and radio programmes of special interest to you.

Remember that you can record television programmes to watch later if you prefer, and check out newspaper headlines online and from sites such as BBC news. The same applies to Podcasts. Of course, to know which information is relevant means that you must be familiar with the content of all the units you are studying, so it is useful to know what topics you will be learning about in the months to come, as well as the ones you are covering now. That way you can recognise useful opportunities when they arise.

Minimising problems

If you are fortunate, any problems you experience on your course will only be minor ones. For example, you may struggle to keep yourself motivated every single day and there may be times that you are having difficulty with a topic. Or you may be struggling to work with someone else in your team or to understand a particular tutor.

During induction you should have been told which tutor to talk to in this situation, and who to see if that person is absent or if you would prefer to see someone else. If you are having difficulties which are distracting you and affecting your work then it is sensible to ask to see your tutor promptly so that you can talk in confidence, rather than just trusting to luck everything will go right again. It is a rare student who is madly enthusiastic about every part of a course and all the other people on the course, so your tutor won't be surprised and will be able to give you useful guidance to help you stay on track.

If you are very unlucky, you may have a more serious personal problem to deal with. In this case it is important that you know the main sources of help in your school or college and how to access these.

- **Professional counselling** There may be a professional counselling service if you have a concern that you don't want to discuss with any teaching staff. If you book an appointment to see a counsellor then you can be certain that nothing you say will ever be mentioned to another member of staff without your permission.

- **Student complaint procedures** If you have a serious complaint to make then the first step is to talk to a tutor, but you should be aware of the formal student complaint procedures that exist if you cannot resolve the problem informally. Note that these are only used for serious issues, not for minor difficulties.

- **Student appeals procedures** If you cannot agree with a tutor about a final grade for an assignment then you need to check the grading criteria and ask the tutor to explain how the grade was awarded. If you are still unhappy then you should see your personal tutor. If you still disagree then you have the right to make a formal appeal.

- **Student disciplinary procedures** These exist so that all students who

The media are invaluable sources of information

flout the rules in a school or college will be dealt with in the same way. Obviously it is wise to avoid getting into trouble at any time, but if you find yourself on the wrong side of the regulations do read the procedures carefully to see what could happen. Remember that being honest about what happened and making a swift apology is always the wisest course of action, rather than being devious or trying to blame someone else.

- **Serious illness** Whether this affects you or a close family member, it could severely affect your attendance. The sooner you discuss the problem with your tutor the better. This is because you will be missing notes and information from the first day you do not attend. Many students under-estimate the ability of their tutors to find inventive solutions in this type of situation – from sending notes by post to updating you electronically if you are well enough to cope with the work.

PLUSPOINTS

+ Some students miss out on opportunities to learn more about relevant topics. This may be because they haven't read the unit specifications, so don't know what topics they will be learning about in future; haven't prepared in advance or don't take advantage of occasions when they can listen to an expert and perhaps ask questions. Examples of these occasions include external visits, visiting speakers, work experience, being at work and watching television.

+ Many students encounter minor difficulties, especially if their course lasts a year or two. It is important to talk to your tutor, or another appropriate person, promptly if you have a worry that is affecting your work.

+ All schools and colleges have procedures for dealing with important issues and problems such as serious complaints, major illnesses, student appeals and disciplinary matters. It is important to know what these are.

ACTION POINTS

✓ List the type of opportunities available on your course for obtaining more information and talking to experts. Then check with your tutor to make sure you haven't missed out any.

✓ Check out the content of each unit you will be studying so that you know the main topics you have still to study.

✓ Identify the type of information you can find on television, in newspapers and in Podcasts that will be relevant to your studies.

✓ Check out your school or college documents and procedures to make sure that you know who to talk to in a crisis and who you can see if the first person is absent.

✓ Find out where you can read a copy of the main procedures in your school or college that might affect you if you have a serious problem. Then do so.

AND FINALLY . . .

Don't expect this Introduction to be of much use if you skim through it quickly and then put it to one side. Instead, refer to it whenever you need to remind yourself about something related to your course.

The same applies to the rest of this Student Guide. The Activities in the next section have been written to help you to demonstrate your understanding of many of the key topics contained in the core or specialist units you are studying. Your tutor may tell you to do these at certain times; otherwise there is nothing to stop you working through them yourself!

Similarly, the Assessed Assignments in the final section have been written to show you how your assignments may be worded. You can also see the type of response that will achieve a Pass, Merit and Distinction – as well as the type of response that won't! Read these carefully and if any comment or grade puzzles you, ask your tutor to explain it.

Then keep this guide in a safe place so that you can use it whenever you need to refresh your memory. That way, you will get the very best out of your course – and yourself!

GLOSSARY

Note: all words highlighted in bold in the text are defined in the glossary.

Accreditation of Prior Learning (APL)

APL is an assessment process that enables your previous achievements and experiences to count towards your qualification providing your evidence is authentic, current, relevant and sufficient.

Apprenticeships

Schemes that enable you to work and earn money at the same time as you gain further qualifications (an **NVQ** award and a technical certificate) and improve your key skills. Apprentices learn work-based skills relevant to their job role and their chosen industry. You can find out more at www.apprenticeships.org.uk/

Assessment methods

Methods, such as **assignments**, case studies and practical tasks, used to check that your work demonstrates the learning and understanding required for your qualification.

Assessor

The tutor who marks or assesses your work.

Assignment

A complex task or mini-project set to meet specific **grading criteria**.

Awarding body

The organisation which is responsible for devising, assessing and issuing qualifications. The awarding body for all BTEC qualifications is Edexcel.

Core units

On a BTEC National course these are the compulsory or mandatory units that all students must complete to gain the qualification. Some BTEC qualifications have an over-arching title, eg Engineering, but within Engineering you can choose different routes. In this case you will study both common core units that are common to all engineering qualifications and **specialist core unit(s)** which are specific to your chosen **pathway**.

Degrees

These are higher education qualifications which are offered by universities and colleges. Foundation degrees take two years to complete; honours degrees may take three years or longer. See also **Higher National Certificates and Diplomas**.

DfES

The Department for Education and Skills: this is the government department responsible for education issues. You can find out more at www.dfes.gov.uk

Distance learning

This enables you to learn and/or study for a qualification without attending an Edexcel centre although you would normally be supported by a member of staff who works there. You communicate with your tutor and/or the centre that organises the distance learning programme by post, telephone or electronically.

Educational Maintenance Award (EMA)

This is a means-tested award which provides eligible students under 19, who arc studying a full-time course at school or college, with a cash sum of money every week. See http://www.dfes.gov.uk/financialhelp/ema/ for up-to-date details.

External verification

Formal checking by a representative of Edexcel of the way a BTEC course is delivered. This includes sampling various assessments to check content and grading.

Final major project

This is a major, individual piece of work that is designed to enable you to demonstrate you have achieved several learning outcomes for a BTEC National qualification in the creative or performing arts. Like all assessments, this is internally assessed.

Forbidden combinations

Qualifications or units that cannot be taken simultaneously because their content is too similar.

GLH

See **Guided Learning Hours** below

Grade

The rating (Pass, Merit or Distinction) given to the mark you have obtained which identifies the standard you have achieved.

Grade boundaries

The pre-set points at which the total points you have earned for different units converts to the overall grade(s) for your qualification.

Grading criteria

The standard you have to demonstrate to obtain a particular grade in the unit, in other words, what you have to prove you can do.

Grading domains

The main areas of learning which support the **learning outcomes**. On a BTEC National course these are: application of knowledge and understanding; development of practical and technical skills; personal development for occupational roles; application of generic and **key skills**. Generic skills are basic skills needed wherever you work, such as the ability to work cooperatively as a member of a team.

Grading grid

The table in each unit of your BTEC qualification specification that sets out the **grading criteria**.

Guided Learning Hours (GLH)

The approximate time taken to deliver a unit which includes the time taken for direct teaching, instruction and assessment and for you to carry out directed assignments or directed individual study. It does not include any time you spend on private study or researching an assignment. The GLH determines the size of the unit. At BTEC National level, units are either 30, 60, 90 or 120 guided learning hours. By looking at the number of GLH a unit takes, you can see the size of the unit and how long it is likely to take you to learn and understand the topics it contains.

Higher education (HE)

Post-secondary and post-further education, usually provided by universities and colleges.

Higher level skills

Skills such as evaluating or critically assessing complex information that are more difficult than lower level skills such as writing a description or making out a list. You must be able to demonstrate higher level skills to achieve a Distinction grade.

Higher National Certificates and Diplomas

Higher National Certificates and Diplomas are vocational qualifications offered at colleges around the country. Certificates are part-time and designed to be studied by people who are already in work; students can use their work experiences to build on their learning. Diplomas are full-time courses – although often students will spend a whole year on work experience part way through their Diploma. Higher Nationals are roughly equivalent to half a degree.

Indicative reading

Recommended books and journals whose content is both suitable and relevant for the unit.

Induction

A short programme of events at the start of a course designed to give you essential information and introduce you to your fellow students and tutors so that you can settle down as quickly and easily as possible.

Internal verification

The quality checks carried out by nominated tutor(s) at your school or college to ensure that all assignments are at the right level and cover appropriate learning outcomes. The checks also ensure that all **assessors** are marking work consistently and to the same standard.

Investors in People (IIP)

A national quality standard which sets a level of good practice for the training and development of people. Organisations must demonstrate their commitment to achieve the standard.

Key skills

The transferable, essential skills you need both at work and to run your own life successfully. They are: literacy, numeracy, IT, problem solving, working with others and self-management.

Learning outcomes

The knowledge and skills you must demonstrate to show that you have effectively learned a unit.

Learning support

Additional help that is available to all students in a school or college who have learning difficulties or other special needs. These include reasonable adjustments to help to reduce the effect of a disability or difficulty that would place a student at a substantial disadvantage in an assessment situation.

Levels of study

The depth, breadth and complexity of knowledge, understanding and skills required to achieve a qualification determines its level. Level 2 is broadly equivalent to GCSE level (grades A*-C) and level 3 equates to GCE level. As you successfully achieve one level, you can then progress on to the next. BTEC qualifications are offered at Entry level, then levels 1, 2, 3, 4 and 5.

Learning and Skills Council (LSC)

The government body responsible for planning and funding education and training for everyone aged over 16 in England - except university students. You can find out more at www.lsc.gov.uk

Local Education Authority (LEA)

The local government body responsible for providing education for students of compulsory school age in your area.

Mentor

A more experienced person who will guide and counsel you if you have a problem or difficulty.

Mode of delivery

The way in which a qualification is offered to students, eg part-time, full-time, as a short course or by **distance learning**.

National Occupational Standard (NOS)

These are statements of the skills, knowledge and understanding you need to develop to be competent at a particular job. These are drawn up by the **Sector Skills Councils**.

National Qualification Framework (NQF)

The framework into which all accredited qualifications in the UK are placed. Each is awarded a level based on their difficulty which ensures that all those at the same level are of the same standard. (See also **levels of study**).

National Vocational Qualification (NVQ)

Qualifications which concentrate upon the practical skills and knowledge required to do a job competently. They are usually assessed in the workplace and range from level 1 (the lowest) to level 5 (the highest).

Nested qualifications

Qualifications which have 'common' units, so that students can easily progress from one to another by adding on more units, such as the BTEC Award, BTEC Certificate and BTEC Diploma.

Pathway

All BTEC National qualifications are comprised of a small number of core units and a larger number of specialist units. These specialist units are grouped into different combinations to provide alternative pathways to achieving the qualification, linked to different career preferences.

Peer review

An occasion when you give feedback on the performance of other members in your team and they, in turn, comment on your performance.

Plagiarism

The practice of copying someone else's work and passing it off as your own. *This is strictly forbidden on all courses.*

Portfolio

A collection of work compiled by a student, usually as evidence of learning to produce for an **assessor**.

Professional body

An organisation that exists to promote or support a particular profession, such as the Law Society and the Royal Institute of British Architects.

Professional development and training

Activities that you can undertake, relevant to your job, that will increase and/or update your knowledge and skills.

Project

A comprehensive piece of work which normally involves original research and investigation either by an individual or a team. The findings and results may be presented in writing and summarised in a presentation.

Qualifications and Curriculum Authority (QCA)

The public body, sponsored by the **DfES**, responsible for maintaining and developing the national curriculum and associated assessments, tests and examinations. It also accredits and monitors qualifications in colleges and at work. You can find out more at www.qca.gov.uk

Quality assurance

In education, this is the process of continually checking that a course of study is meeting the specific requirements set down by the awarding body.

Sector Skills Councils (SSCs)

The 25 employer-led, independent organisations that are responsible for improving workforce skills in the UK by identifying skill gaps and improving learning in the workplace. Each council covers a different type of industry and develops its **National Occupational Standards**.

Semester

Many universities and colleges divide their academic year into two halves or semesters, one from September to January and one from February to July.

Seminar

A learning event between a group of students and a tutor. This may be student-led, following research into a topic which has been introduced earlier.

Specialist core units

See under **Core units**.

Study buddy

A person in your group or class who takes notes for you and keeps you informed of important developments if you are absent. You do the same in return.

Time-constrained assignment

An assessment you must complete within a fixed time limit.

Tutorial

An individual or small group meeting with your tutor at which you can discuss the work you are currently doing and other more general course issues. At an individual tutorial your progress on the course will be discussed and you can also raise any concerns or personal worries you have.

The University and Colleges Admissions Service (UCAS)

The central organisation which processes all applications for higher education courses. You pronounce this 'You-Cass'.

UCAS points

The number of points allocated by **UCAS** for the qualifications you have obtained. **HE** institutions specify how many points you need to be accepted on the courses they offer. You can find out more at www.ucas.com

Unit abstract

The summary at the start of each BTEC unit that tells you what the unit is about.

Unit content

Details about the topics covered by the unit and the knowledge and skills you need to complete it.

Unit points

The number of points you have gained when you complete a unit. These depend upon the grade you achieve (Pass, Merit or Distinction) and the size of the unit as determined by its **guided learning hours**.

Vocational qualification

A qualification which is designed to develop the specific knowledge and understanding relevant to a chosen area of work.

Work experience

Any time you spend on an employer's premises when you carry out work-based tasks as an employee but also learn about the enterprise and develop your skills and knowledge.

ACTIVITIES

This section focuses on grading criteria P1, P2, P3, P5; M1 and M3 and aspects of D1 from Unit 1 'Exploring Business Activity'.

Learning outcomes

1 Understand the different types of business activity and ownership.

2 Understand how the type of business influences the setting of strategic aims and objectives.

4 Know how external factors in the business environment impact on organisations.

Content

1) **Understand the different types of business activity and ownership**

Types of business activity: local; national; international; global; public, private; not-for-profit/voluntary; sectors of business (primary, secondary and tertiary)

Business purposes: reasons why businesses exist; how products and services may be supplied for profit, at cost and below cost by local, national and global business organisations; how businesses supply products and services to consumers, other businesses, and central and local government agencies in response to demand

Owners: public, private and voluntary sectors; types of ownership, eg sole trader, partnerships, private and public limited companies, franchises, government departments, government agencies, worker cooperatives, charitable trusts

Key stakeholders: customers; employees, suppliers; owners; pressure groups; trade unions; employer associations; local and national communities; governments; links and interdependencies.

2) **Understand how the type of business influences the setting of strategic aims and objectives**

Strategic planning process: quantitative and qualitative analysis of current situation; setting aims and objectives; planning strategies

Public and voluntary sector strategies: service provision; public sector services; eg primary health care trusts; voluntary sector services; service level agreements; quality assurance; provision at below or at cost

Private sector strategies: profit maximisation; sales; products' services at cost profit; increasing revenue and cutting costs; break-even; survival; marketing; competitors

Growth: profit; sales; market share.

4) **Know how external factors in the business environment impact on organisations**

Political factors: national and international law, eg employment, contracts, consumer rights, environmental issues, fraud; government, eg taxation and subsidies

Economic factors: pay levels; cost of credit; competitive pressures; globalisation markets; labour, supply and demand; energy prices

Social factors: eg ageing population, hosting of major sporting or cultural events, celebrity culture

Technological factors: increased access to broadband; telephony developments

Impact: new organisations; winding up of existing organisations, take-overs and mergers; revision of strategic plans; impact on stakeholders; functional activity changes.

Grading criteria

P1 describe the type of business, purpose and ownership of two contrasting organisations

'Contrasting' is the same as 'comparing' and you can only do this effectively if you choose two organisations that are very different in what they do and how they are owned.

P2 describe the different stakeholders who influence the purpose of two contrasting organisations

This means you need to know which stakeholders are the most powerful, and why. Remember this varies between organisations!

P3 outline the rationale of the strategic aims and objectives of two contrasting organisations

This means that you have to explain the reason why each organisation has chosen those aims and objectives.

M1 explain the points of view from different stakeholders seeking to influence the strategic aims and objectives of two contrasting organisations

Do this effectively by thinking about the situation from the viewpoint of each different stakeholder. Do this by identifying the interests of each one and what they hope to achieve.

P5 describe how three external factors are impacting upon the business activities of the selected organisations and their stakeholders

Remember that external factors are those which are outside the control of the business.

M3 analyse how external factors have impacted on the two contrasting organisations

This means that you will need to identify the appropriate external factors in each case and then assess their effect on that business.

ACTIVITY 1

TYPES OF BUSINESS ACTIVITY

There are many different businesses in your area. Each one will undertake a particular type of business activity for a specific purpose.

Task 1

Businesses vary in many ways – in the scale of their operations, how they are owned and the type of activities they carry out. This can mean they are classified into different sectors.

Check that you understand the meaning of all these terms by categorising each of the following well-known businesses correctly in the table at the top of the next page. To help, the first one is done for you.

Task 2

Now apply what you know to your own area. Using a table similar to the one on the next page list ten completely different types of business that operate in your locality. For each one, write down what the business does and whether it provides a product or a service.

Then analyse each business in three ways:

- Decide the scale of its operations, ie whether it operates at local, national, international or global level
- Decide its ownership, ie whether it is in the public, private, or voluntary sector
- Decide the sector of business in which each one operates, ie primary, secondary or tertiary.

  Write your ideas in the table on the next page.

As a class, compare your ideas. Then check that you have an example to represent each variation in terms of scale, ownership and business sector.

41

Business organisation	Scale of operations ie local, national, international or global	Ownership ie public, private or voluntary sector	Business sector ie primary, secondary, tertiary sector
Toyota	Global	Private	Secondary
Tesco			
Oxfam			
BBC			
Kelloggs			
British Coal			
HSBC			
Your council			
TUC			
NHS Direct			

Business organisation	What it does	Scale of operations	Ownership	Business sector

ACTIVITY 2

BUSINESS PURPOSES

All businesses exist for a reason – usually to provide goods or services. However, the way in which they supply these and the prices they charge can be very different, as you will see as you do the tasks that follow.

Task 1

Some items are priced so that the suppliers cover the costs of production and supply and make a profit as their reward for their efforts and investment. Others may be supplied free or priced just to cover the cost of supply.

Business	Main purpose	Main pricing strategy	Reason
M&S plc	High street retailer	Sells goods for profit	To reward the owners (shareholders) and provide money for future investment and expansion.
Your college			
UNICEF			
Manchester University			
Topshop			
Passport Office			
UNISON			
Connexions			
Your doctor			
A local vet			
Fire service			
Microsoft			
Greenpeace			
Chelsea FC			

a) The table on the previous page lists several well-known businesses or types of business. **On your own**, identify the main purpose of the business, ie what it does and its main pricing strategy – whether it normally supplies its goods or services for profit, at cost or below cost.

b) **In groups of two or three**, compare your answers and see if you agree. Then decide on the main reason for the pricing strategy of each business. To help, the first one is done for you.

c) **In your group**, add three more examples of your own. Ideally, each should pursue a different type of pricing strategy.

d) Compare your ideas **with other members of your class**.

Task 2

Imran received an Xbox 360 for Christmas. To his horror he found that games for it were around £49.99 (the Recommended Retail Price) in some local high street game stores. Then he discovered he could buy them a little bit cheaper online and in some large high street stores, such as John Lewis. But then he noticed he could save more money if he bought them at Tesco, where some games were only £29. Alternatively he could look on eBay to see if he could find any bargains.

Working in small groups, decide your answers to the following questions. Then compare your ideas **with other groups in your class**.

a) You are the owners of a local high street games store. You buy X360 games for £25 each. What factors will influence your decision to sell the games at their RRP or not?

b) Identify four reasons why online stores and high street stores like John Lewis may be able to sell the games more cheaply than a local games store.

c) You suddenly see that Tesco is promoting a new game both online and in its stores for only £15! You think that it couldn't possibly have purchased the games so cheaply. Explain why Tesco is prepared to make a loss on each of the games that it sells.

d) The business purpose of eBay is different from that of other mainstream retailers who sell online, such as Amazon or John Lewis.

    i) Explain the main business purpose of a retailer such as Amazon or John Lewis.

    ii) Explain the main business purpose of eBay. In your answer say how this enables buyers to obtain a bargain and yet keeps sellers happy at the same time!

Task 3

The main business purpose of your local council is to provide services for the local community – and council tax is one of the main methods of financing this. Every year though, councils argue that they need more money and need to increase the amount they raise, usually above the rate of inflation. This has meant that many people now find it very difficult to pay.

To make matters worse, a revaluation of all properties in England is long overdue, although this probably won't take place until after the next General Election. This would take into account home improvements that have been made as well as the rise in property values since the last valuation in 1991. It would be likely to result in a substantial increase in revenue for councils, over and above any annual increases.

In addition, Sir Michael Lyons' report in 2007 proposed a new top rate tax band for the most expensive properties and a new bottom rate for the cheapest, as well as suggesting additional help for pensioners and other ways of raising money for councils.

The Taxpayers' Alliance called the report 'a missed opportunity' arguing that it would allow councils to waste even more money than they do at the moment.

a) There are three other ways in which councils receive revenue besides council tax. Find out what these are and list them.

b) Find out how much money your own council raised in council tax last year by accessing its website.

c) All councils provide many services. Use your council's website to find out what it spends its money on. Then list the services on which it spends the most money.

d) Sir Michael Lyons wants to do more to help pensioners. Why do so many of this group have problems paying their council tax bills?

e) Sir Michael Lyons' report was commissioned by Gordon Brown and John Prescott in 2004, but is unlikely to be acted upon until after the next General Election. Can you suggest why?

f) Councils argue that they need more money to improve their services. Local people may argue that some money is wasted and their council is not very efficient.

Find out how efficient your council is by accessing the council league tables produced by the Audit Commission at http://www.auditcommission.gov.uk/cpa/.

g) Divide into two groups to debate the issue 'Increased council tax results in improved services for the local community'. One group should argue the case for raising additional money; the other must list and present arguments against it. Try to keep your arguments rational and not emotional! Your tutor will decide which side wins the debate.

ACTIVITY 3

BUSINESS OWNERSHIP

There are many different types of business ownership. You need to understand how these differ and the circumstances under which each one is most appropriate.

Task 1

Working in a small group:

a) Complete the table on the next page by writing a brief definition to explain each of the following types of business owners. Then identify two or three examples of each one.

b) On nine separate post-it notes, one for each type of 'owner', copy the names of your examples. Do NOT put a heading.

c) Exchange your nine post-it notes with another group.

d) Pin up nine pages of A1 flip chart paper. On each put the name of a different type of owner.

e) Correctly identify the owners of each post-it note you have received and stick them on the correct piece of flipchart paper. See if your class can group all the examples under the right headings with no mistakes! Then check that you all agree on your definitions.

Owners	Definition	Examples
Sole trader		
Partnership		
Private limited company		
Public limited company		
Franchise		
Government department		
Government agencies		
Worker cooperatives		
Charitable trusts		

Task 2

Jack and Joanna are both determined to work for themselves and have been identifying business opportunities in their area. They are convinced that an excellent, professional cleaning service would be very successful, especially if they could obtain both business and domestic customers. They know that they will need to recruit and manage a team of reliable workers as well as undertake all the administrative work required. They consider, though, that their start-up costs would be quite reasonable, so that their initial investment would not be too high.

At this stage they are trying to work out what type of ownership would be best. They have listed their options as follows:

Ownership options

1 Both set up separately as sole traders
2 Set up together in a partnership
3 Start a private limited company
4 Start a franchise with an established organisation like Molly Maid (see http://www.mollymaid.co.uk/business/)
5 Recruit other similar-minded people into a worker cooperative.

Working in small groups, decide which type of ownership would best suit their business purpose. Do this by identifying the main advantages and disadvantages of each option and then relate each one to the main purpose of their business. Use websites such as www.businesslink.gov.uk and http://www.lloydstsbbusiness.com/support/businessguides/what_type_of_business.asp (as well as other banking websites) to help you. You can also find out more about cleaning services online, such as at www.wesparkle.co.uk and www.keephouse.biz.

When you have completed your investigations, make a short presentation to your class explaining your group's decision and giving appropriate reasons for your preferred choice. Explain, too, why you rejected the other options.

Task 3

The closure of the village shop has often sounded the death knell for many small rural communities. Yet village shops struggle to compete with large supermarkets who set up in business in nearby towns. This obviously deters potential entrepreneurs who may have been tempted to set up on their own in such a venture.

An alternative, for communities who are determined to retain or introduce a local shop is community ownership. In this case the business may be owned by its intended customers, by members of the community or by a range of stakeholders.

Obviously, any community considering such a venture needs expert advice. ViRSA – Village Retail Services Association – does just this. ViRSA is part of the Plunkett Foundation – a charity which helps rural communities to adapt and change. It provides free advice and assistance via its website and through its network of advisers. It advises communities on every aspect of setting up in business, from legal aspects of ownership and writing the business plan to obtaining funding from different sources, such as the parish council, the local bank or DEFRA – the Department of Environment, Food and Rural Affairs. ViRSA's shop directory currently lists over 150 community-owned shops now trading successfully in England, Scotland and Wales.

a) Suggest the most likely form of ownership for each of the following organisations mentioned in the article above:

   i) The traditional village shop
   ii) A large national supermarket
   iii) DEFRA
   iv) The parish council
   v) ViRSA
   vi) A village shop owned by its customers.

b) Explain why village shops struggle to compete with large supermarkets.

c) ViRSA advises that the structure of a community-owned shop should not give ownership according to the level of investment made by different stakeholders. The reason is because this is only appropriate for enterprises that intend to maximise the return on the investment of the owners.

i) Identify the most usual type of business organisation where ownership is directly related to the level of investment, ie the more you own, the more control you have.

ii) Find out more about successful community owned shops on the ViRSA website. Then explain in your own words why the type of ownership outlined in i) above would be inappropriate in this situation.

ACTIVITY 4

KEY STAKEHOLDERS

As a student you are a key stakeholder in your college, so too is your tutor. Often stakeholders can influence the behaviour of a business, but not always – as you will see below!

Task 1

In March 2007 Blackburn Rovers football team announced that it was going to give some of its share of the new premiership TV deal, amounting to £35 million, back to its fans by using the money to reduce ticket prices at its home ground, Ewood Park.

This will substantially reduce the cost of a season ticket and, with reduced junior prices too, will bring the price of home premiership matches back within the reach of most families in the area.

Rovers have admitted that they are doing this because match day attendances have been declining. Some other premiership teams don't have this problem, of course. So you can expect clubs like Chelsea and Manchester United to put their share towards buying more top players instead.

Working in groups of two or three, decide upon your answers to the following questions:

a) Supporters are a key stakeholder of all football clubs. Write a list of all the other stakeholders you can identify for a premiership club. Brainstorm this, so that you get as many as you can.

b) Identify which of the stakeholders in your list are **key** to the operations of a club. Remember that this means that they have the ability (or power) to influence the way in which the club operates. In each case give a reason for your choice.

c) Shareholder A agrees with Rovers' decision to spend its share on reducing prices. Shareholder B disagrees and thinks that new players would give better value for money. Shareholder C cannot decide – but also holds the view that some of the facilities need to be improved.

Take the role of one of these shareholders and present a convincing and persuasive argument to influence the others of your case.

Task 2

South West Trains (SWT) had a bumpy ride at the start of 2007. First it was accused of the worst overcrowding on the rail network, after removing carriages from its trains to save money. Its response was to remove seats and lavatories on its busiest routes to create more standing room. Then it announced a price rise of up to 20% for passengers who travel to London after the morning rush hour.

This news came hot on the heels of the announcement that the Chief Executive of Stagecoach (which owns SWT), Brian Souter, and his sister Ann Gloag, are to benefit from a £100 million windfall as part of a share buy-back deal. This will be their share of the £400 million cash which will be returned to all Stagecoach shareholders before June.

Anthony Smith, Chief Executive of Passenger Focus, accused SWT of 'exploiting its monopoly market' with an 'unjustified, unexplained and unfair price hike'. He was also concerned that other companies may follow suit. This is not surprising as the Department for Transport (DfT) has already admitted that it approved SWT's plans to increase these fares last year when Stagecoach bid £1.2 billion to renew its franchise for Britain's busiest route. The DfT argued that as these related to increases in cheap day return fares, which are unregulated, the company had commercial freedom to decide what price to charge.

SWT said the increase was necessary to match demand and pricing more accurately. Too many people were catching the first off-peak train and good savings were still available to anyone who wanted to travel later in the day.

Gerry Doherty, General Secretary of the transport union TSSA disagreed, arguing that the increase amounted to 'daylight robbery', particularly in view of Stagecoach's profit levels. Stagecoach would argue that profits are vital. It is well aware of the fate of the Great North Eastern Railway (GNER) which lost its franchise last year after getting into financial difficulties. The DfT has made it quite clear that any operator that does this should expect to surrender its franchise.

Working in small groups, answer the following questions. Research online to find out any information that you don't already know.

a) i) What is a rail franchise?

ii) Why do you think operators are keen to run one?

iii) Operators 'bid' to get a franchise when one becomes available. Explain what this means.

b) In your own words, explain what is meant by the following phrases in the article:

i) 'a share buy-back deal'

49

ii) 'a monopoly market'

iii) 'commercial freedom to decide what price to charge'

iv) 'match demand and pricing more accurately'.

c) List all the stakeholders mentioned in the article. For each one, identify their major area of interest in the issue.

d) i) Identify two stakeholders which act as pressure groups.

ii) In January 2007, First Great Western passengers took part in a fares boycott to protest about late and overcrowded trains. The protest group More Trains Less Strain estimated that more than 2,000 passengers took part. How effective do you think this type of action is by passengers? Give a reason for your answer.

iii) Passengers can get together now online to protest in online forums, such as http://railforums.co.uk/ and http://railwaysonline.co.uk/. Do you think this just gives an extra outlet for passenger anger, or can it be used to put pressure on train operators more effectively? Give a reason for your answer.

e) Some people claim that the train network has never been the same since it was privatised by John Major's Conservative government in 1994. After the Paddington rail crash, a Guardian/ICM poll found that 73% of voters would support re-nationalisation. Divide into two groups in your class to debate the following issue: The need to make healthy profits means rail passengers are at best inconvenienced and at worst actively in danger when they travel.

Task 3

In 2002, Ofcom complained that Channel 4 was becoming too mainstream and wasn't pursuing its core aims of creativity, originality, individuality and diversity. It recommended that the channel should concentrate more on distinctive programmes that included minority opinions.

No one can argue that Channel 4 didn't do that when *Celebrity Big Brother* was broadcast in January 2007! Indeed, perhaps that is one reason why it was so slow to take action over the treatment dished out by Jade Goody, Jo O'Meara and Danielle Lloyd to Shilpa Shetty. Or – as some of the 50,000 viewers who complained thought – perhaps it was because it didn't want to risk losing its massively increased viewing figures.

Whatever the reason, the crisis reverberated around the world and Channel 4's management was accused of condoning racism. Gordon Brown, the Chancellor of the Exchequer, who was visiting India on a trade visit at the same time, was besieged with questions about the row. Ofcom announced an investigation to find out if Channel 4 was guilty of breaching programme codes and Carphone Warehouse backed out as Big Brother sponsor. Jade, Jo and Danielle were evicted from the house – and Shilpa Shetty won.

Was the row staged? Did Channel 4 drag its feet to keep its viewing figures? Will Ofcom, the regulator, find Channel 4 guilty of breaching programme codes? Is it the end of *Big Brother* – or Jade Goody? Or has the whole thing been a (media manufactured) storm in a teacup?

The cast and players

Channel 4 – the broadcaster. *Big Brother* is its most profitable programme because it normally obtains about £70 million in advertising revenue as well as sponsorship money. Promised to hold an internal enquiry.

Kevin Lygo – Channel 4 Director of Television. He admitted before racism row he wanted to enliven the series.

Andy Duncan – Chief Executive of Channel 4. Lygo's boss.

Channel 4 board – expressed regret about the row and confidence in Mr Duncan.

Endemol – the programme's producer.

Ofcom – the media regulator – announced investigation into the row.

Gordon Brown – Chancellor of the Exchequer at the time of the row, predicted to be the next Labour Prime Minister.

Shilpa Shetty – Bollywood actress at centre of racism row. Her dignified response has helped to boost her career.

Jade Goody – former dental nurse who shot to fame after her appearance in *Big Brother* in 2002 when the tabloids mocked her lack of general knowledge.

John Noel – Goody's agent – also agent of several other winners and manager of presenter Davina McCall and others.

Davina McCall – *Big Brother* presenter. Accused of giving Jade Goody and the others an easy ride when she interviewed them after they were evicted.

Danielle Lloyd – model, one of the footballers' WAGs, former Miss Britain.

Jo O'Meara – former S Club singer.

Carphone Warehouse – *Big Brother* sponsor since 2004 at an estimated cost of £3 million. Pulled out as a result of the row.

HarperCollins – pulled paperback publication of Goody's autobiography as a result of the row. The hardback version made £1 million.

Boots, Debenhams, The Perfume Shop – stopped stocking Goody's perfume following the row.

Lucie Cave – ghost writer of Goody's autobiography. Works as Features Editor for *Heat* magazine. *Heat* was the only magazine to interview Jade when she left the BB house. Its continued coverage of her resulted in online petitions in protest.

The police and Crown Prosecution Service – after investigation announced that scenes were 'offensive but not criminal'.

51

Was it good to get everyone discussing the allegations of racist bullying and the issues that surround it? Was Carphone Warehouse over-reacting and will another sponsor just replace it? Should Ofcom forget the whole thing? Has it all worked out fairly in the end, especially given the boost to Shilpa Shetty's career?

What do you think?

Your tasks

a) **Work in a small group** to identify the key areas of interest for each of the stakeholders listed on the previous page at the time the row took place and how this affected their actions and behaviour.

b) Then identify the KEY stakeholders who were directly involved in the furore.

c) Take the role of ONE key stakeholder and be prepared to explain his or her points of view to influence the future aims and objectives of the *Big Brother* programme.

d) Find out whether the row had any effect on *Big Brother*'s format or output – and what Ofcom eventually decided by researching online to see what happened next!

ACTIVITY 5

STRATEGIC AIMS AND OBJECTIVES

The aims and objectives of a business state what the business intends to do in the future. These will differ depending upon the type of organisation and what it wants to achieve. You need to understand how the type of business will influence the setting of both the aims and objectives.

Task 1

M&S has announced Plan A – its five-year, £200 million business-wide eco-plan containing five major commitments and 100 changes it wants to make. These will affect all aspects of its operations.

Its commitments focus around five areas:

- Climate change
- Waste
- Sustainable raw materials
- Being a fair partner (to its suppliers and local communities)
- Health.

M&S argues there is no 'Plan B' because we only have one world. It has been advised by Forum for the Future and its proposals have been praised by both Greenpeace UK and WWF-UK. By 2012 it intends to:

- Become carbon neutral
- Send no waste to landfill
- Extend sustainable sourcing
- Set new standards in ethical trading
- Help customers and employees live a healthier lifestyle.

Find out more at www.marksandspencer.com/PlanA and then answer the questions that follow.

a) List in full the five major aims of Plan A.

b) Identify any five SMART objectives relating to these aims.

c) Identify any two objectives where you think achievement may be more difficult to measure. Give a reason for your choices.

d) Why do you think M&S has adopted this strategy?

e) In what ways do you think different M&S stakeholders may be affected? Remember that to answer this question you will need to identify key stakeholders first.

f) Over the previous few years, M&S focused on improving its business after it lost sales to its major competitors. Stuart Rose, the Chief Executive is widely credited with turning around the business since 2003. Suggest what his strategies would have been at that time, when he was setting the aims and objectives.

Compare your ideas **with other members of your class**.

Task 2

If you like the outdoor life then you're probably a fan of Fat Face, the lifestyle retail business set up by Tim Slade and Jules Leaver – originally to fund their love of skiing.

Fat Face has grown rapidly from its lowly beginnings in 1988. In 2007 it had 128 retail stores in the UK, Ireland and France. Since 2002 it has opened an average of 17 new stores every year. It has also opened franchise stores in Dubai and Iceland.

In 2005, Slade and Leaver sold the business to a private equity firm, Advent International, for £100 million but kept a 30% stake. Their management team also owned 16% of the business.

In 2007 the business was sold again, to Bridgepoint, a European private equity group for £360 million, thanks to its healthy profit figures. In 2005 sales rocketed by 33% and then in 2006 by a further 38%, to £51.7 million in the six months to the end of November. Operating profits were a record £9 million for the same period.

Fat Face has no intention of standing still in the future. By 2010–11 it intends to have 190 stores and is currently collaborating with John Lewis to sell the Fat Face brand in 20 of its stores. It plans to open stores in the Middle East, Hong Kong, Singapore, Russia and Canada. It also has a licence to market the brand in Australia and New Zealand.

Additional plans include expanding its product lines, focusing mainly on children's wear, small sizes and beachwear. It intends to increase its turnover from £111 million in the 2006–07 financial year to £214 million by 2010–11.

It will continue to be run by its management team, CEO Louise Barnes and Finance Director Stuart Owens, both of whom are reinvesting in the business.

Either **on your own,** or **working in a small group,** use your knowledge of business to answer the following questions. Research any answers you do not know. Then compare your ideas **with other members of your group.**

a) What share of the Fat Face business did Advent hold at the start of 2007?

b) Who has control of Fat Face now – Advent, Bridgepoint, the founders or the management team – and why?

c) Is Fat Face a successful business? Support your decision with appropriate evidence from the article.

d) What is the difference between an ordinary Fat Face store and a franchise store?

e) Private equity firms buy companies to make a return on their investment. They may hold the company for the long term; alternatively they may make management changes and sell the company on quite quickly. Did Advent make a profit on the deal – and if so, roughly how much?

f) The Fat Face philosophy is 'Life is out there'. Identify six key objectives it has set to fulfil this vision.

g) Explain what you consider was Fat Face's rationale when it set these objectives.

h) Find out about Fat Face's current financial performance at www.fatface.com. If you have completed Unit 2, you will be able to analyse its sales and profits more precisely!

Task 3

Businesses in the private sector decide their own aims and objectives. Public limited companies are mainly accountable to their shareholders for their performance in terms of achieving financial and other targets, although the financial press often highlights their results. In a private limited company, performance is just between the owners and the taxman!

Businesses in the public sector are rather different. Because they are funded from taxation, they are accountable to everyone. This means that they must publish their aims, objectives and targets. They can also expect the media to take an active interest in their performance and to highlight any problems!

This is particularly the case when it comes to the Government. Not only the media, but also other political parties, are ready to pounce on any shortfalls. They have plenty of scope because the Government publishes its Public Service Agreement (PSA) targets. These state:

- The key aims and objectives of all government departments
- Outcome-focused performance targets to deliver further improvements in key areas of public service delivery
- 'Floor' targets which focus in particular on areas of deprivation
- 'Standards' to ensure that when targets are met they are sustained or improved.

As an example, the aim, objectives and performance targets of HM Revenue and Customs are shown opposite.

Carry out this task **in groups of two or three**.

a) HM Revenue and Customs has a major influence over the lives of every person and every business in the UK. Can you say why?

b) Read through the aims and objectives of HM Revenue and Customs. Check you can identify the separate performance

HM REVENUE AND CUSTOMS
AIM

Administer the tax and customs control systems fairly and efficiently and make it as easy as possible for individuals and businesses to understand and comply with their obligations and receive their tax credits and other entitlements.

OBJECTIVES AND PERFORMANCE TARGETS

Objective I: Improve the extent to which individuals and businesses pay the amount of tax due and receive the credits and payments to which they are entitled.

1 *By 2007–08, reduce the scale of VAT losses to no more than 11% of the theoretical liability.*

2 *By 2007–08:*

- *Reduce the illicit market share for cigarettes to no more than 13%*
- *Reduce the illicit market share for spirits by at least a half*
- *Hold the illicit market share for oils in England, Scotland and Wales at no more than 2%.*

3 By 2007–08, reduce underpayment of direct tax and national insurance contributions due by at least £3 billion a year.

4 By 2007–08, increase the percentage of individuals who file their Self-Assessment returns on time to at least 93%.

Objective II: Improve customer experience, support business and reduce the compliance burden.

Objective III: Strengthen frontier protection against threats to the security, social and economic integrity and environment of the United Kingdom in a way that balances the need to maintain the UK as a competitive location in which to do business.

targets. Then work through the document and highlight any words or phrases you do not understand. Then, **as a class**, discuss these so that everyone is clear about their meanings.

c) All Public Service Agreements 2005–08 are available online as pdf files at http://www.hm-treasury.gov.uk/spending_review/spend_sr04/spend_sr04_index.cfm. The full list is shown overleaf. In agreement with your tutor, identify at least one agreement for your group to research. This means downloading the pdf file(s) and then summarising it so that you can clearly explain the aims, objectives and performance targets of that department to the rest of your class.

d) **As a class**, decide how the strategies and rationale behind setting aims and objectives are different between the public and the private sectors.

e) HM Treasury is currently working on the 2007 Comprehensive Spending Review focusing on departmental targets for 2008–11.

You can see if you can do better than the Chancellor, online at http://csr07.treasury.gov.uk/simulation/index.aspx and compare how you would spend taxpayers' money compared with other groups in your class!

PUBLIC SERVICE AGREEMENTS 2005–08

Department for Education and Skills

Department of Health

Department for Transport

Office of the Deputy Prime Minister

Home Office

Department for Constitutional Affairs

Crown Prosecution Service

Ministry of Defence

Foreign and Commonwealth Office

Department for International Development

Department of Trade and Industry

Department for Environment, Food and Rural Affairs

Department for Culture, Media and Sport

Department for Work and Pensions

Northern Ireland Office

HM Treasury

HM Revenue and Customs

Cabinet Office

The Criminal Justice System

Action against Illegal Drugs

ACTIVITY 6

EXTERNAL FACTORS IN THE BUSINESS ENVIRONMENT

All businesses are affected by external events in one way or another. A change which benefits one business may be a serious threat to another. You need to understand the type of changes that affect business, the impact these can have and the way in which businesses may respond.

Task 1

a) Major changes affect all businesses. The table opposite summarises some typical changes that affect the business world. Your task is to decide how it would affect the type of business listed and what this business might do in response. Then identify a type of business that would be affected in a different way – and say why.

b) Suggest four changes, and businesses, of your own to add to the table (below), to represent (one each) a political, economic, social and technological factor.

Compare your answers **as a class**.

Change	Business	Impact and response	Different example
Energy prices rise substantially	Manufacturing company		
Interest rates increase	Estate agent		
England to host World Cup 2018	Sportswear retailer		
30 MB broadband connections announced	DVD rental company		
Major security glitch identified with Windows Vista	Bank		
Education spending increased in budget	Educational publisher		
Major scandal involving football celebrity	Magazine publisher		
Flexible working rights for all working mothers are introduced	Small firm of accountants		
Chancellor increases tax on gas-guzzling vehicles	Car manufacturer		

Task 2

Mergers or takeovers are often one result of change as businesses consolidate to improve their chances of survival or become more competitive. This was the rationale behind the shake-up among the UK's largest tour operators in 2007. In a matter of weeks the 'Big Four' became two. My Travel and Thomas Cook were the first to announce a £3 billion tie-up and estimated this would enable their annual costs to be cut by £75 million as a result.

Hot on the heels of this announcement came the news that Thomson Holidays and First Choice were to join forces in a £4.5 billion merger which is expected to result in savings of £100 million a year. According to the new chief executive, Peter Long, the rationale is to run the business more efficiently without putting up prices.

In groups of two or three, decide your answers to the following questions. Then compare your ideas **with other members of your class**.

a) Suggest four ways in which the new, merged travel companies are likely to be able to make the savings they want to achieve.

b) Package holiday firms have had to face new types of competition and changes in their customers' buying behaviour over the past ten years. Using the main headings of Political, Economic, Social and Technological to help you, identify the main changes that have affected the package tour travel business in recent years.

c) Do you think the mergers are good news or bad news for the travelling public? Give a reason for your answer.

Task 3

The effect of technological changes on the music industry has been even more dramatic than in the travel business. Tower Records, a huge American retail chain, closed its doors in 2006 and Music Zone, the UK's third largest music and film retailer, followed suit after disastrous Christmas sales. Is Britain's largest music retailer, HMV, about to meet the same fate?

THE FANTASTIC MR FOX?

Fox was appointed Chief Executive of the HMV Group (which includes both HMV and Waterstones) in September 2006. He is experienced, confident and optimistic that his three-year turnaround plan will save the company. This is despite the fact that in March 2007 the business issued its second profit warning in three months.

HMV's problems stem from poor sales of CDs and DVDs as a result of the growth in the download market, competition from Amazon and the buying power of large supermarkets.

Simon Fox and his board have identified three key areas on which they intend to focus to revolutionise the business:

- Cutting costs by £40 million a year until 2010 by simplifying the supply chain for both HMV and Waterstones and buying in bulk

- Revitalising the core business by selling MP3 players in HMV and stationery at Waterstones; revamping the HMV store format to include juice bars and gaming areas; introducing a loyalty card

- Establishing new channels to include a social networking site for music, film and game enthusiasts; partnering mobile phone company 3 to provide content to its subscribers; increasing marketing across the stores.

The cost of the new initiatives will be financed by reducing new store openings. You can find further details on the strategic and operational review of the company at http://www.hmvgroup.com/media/view.jsp?id=1157.

a) Read the article on the previous page and, **first in small groups and then as a class**, discuss how effective Simon Fox's new strategy is likely to be, based on the challenges faced by HMV.

b) Suggest any further changes he could make to improve his chances of success.

c) Check out the current situation at HMV by researching online to see how successful Mr Fox has been so far.

This section focuses on grading criteria P3, P4, P5, P6; M2, M3; and D2 from Unit 2 'Investigating Business Resources'.

Learning outcomes

3 Understand how to access sources of finance.

4 Be able to interpret financial statements.

Content

3) **Understand how to access sources of finance**

Internal sources: owner's savings; capital from profits

External sources: banks, eg overdraft, business loan; commercial mortgage; venture capital; hire purchase; leasing; factoring; share issues.

4) **Be able to interpret financial statements**

Costs and budgets: costs managed to budget (fixed costs/variable costs, breakeven, monitoring budgets and variances); income increased to budget; bidding to increase future resources, eg capital grants, investment; provision of appropriate liquidity/working capital; provision of appropriate reserves to address emergencies/crises

Financial statements: profit and loss (purpose and use, measure of trading performance, establishing profit figures) and balance sheet (purpose and use, establishing net worth, measure and business valuation)

Basic ratios: to determine solvency, eg current ratio, acid test ratio; to determine profitability, eg gross profit percentage; net profit percentage; return of capital employed; to determine performance, eg stock turnover, debtors' collection period, asset turnover.

Grading criteria

P3 describe where sources of finance can be obtained for starting up a selected business

This means identifying appropriate sources of finance for the business you have chosen and stating where each one can be obtained.

P4 give the reasons why costs and budgets need to be controlled

You will need to give specific examples of costs that a business can incur and show that you can identify problems that can occur with budgets and suggest appropriate remedies.

P5 interpret the contents of a given profit and loss account and balance sheet

Your interpretation should include your comments on the contents of the statement and an explanation of the purpose of each element. You should also say whether you think the business is viable although, to achieve P5, you do not need to give reasons for your opinion.

P6 illustrate the financial state of a given business by showing examples of accounting ratios

This means using appropriate accounting ratios to check the viability of the business and then describing your results. Remember to show both the formula and your workings.

M2 analyse the reasons why costs and budgets need to be controlled and explain in detail problems that can arise if they are left unmonitored

This means developing your answer to P4 by breaking down a budget into its individual components and identifying why it may be overspent. This means explaining the reasons why this can happen as well as suggesting the best way(s) of rectifying the problem.

M3 interpret the contents of a given profit and loss account and balance sheet and explain in detail how accounting ratios can be used to monitor the financial state of the organisation

This extends your answers to P5 and P6 but now you must use accounting ratios to decide how well the business is doing as well as its performance in its own sector. You will need to provide detailed information about the ratios you have chosen and how they have helped you to form a judgement about the business.

This develops M3 and you will need to make a judgement about the usefulness of the ratios you have used explaining their benefits and any drawbacks in that particular situation.

D2 evaluate the adequacy of accounting ratios as a means of monitoring business health in a selected organisation, using examples

ACTIVITY 1

UNDERSTAND HOW TO ACCESS SOURCES OF FINANCE

All businesses need finance, particularly when they are starting up. You need to understand about the different types of finance that are available and where to access these.

Task 1

Work in groups of two or three for the first part of this task.

a) Write a definition for each of the type of finance listed below:
  i) Owner's savings
  ii) Capital from profits
  iii) Overdraft
  iv) Business loan
  v) Commercial mortgage
  vi) Venture capital
  vii) Hire purchase
  viii) Leasing
  ix) Factoring
  x) Share issue

b) Identify whether each type of finance would come from an internal or external source.

c) Suggest one advantage and one disadvantage for a business obtaining each type of finance.

As a group present your ideas to the rest of the class.

Listen to the other groups presenting their findings and, after each one, contribute to suggesting improvements to the information provided.

Task 2

Entrepreneurs with financial needs

Rizwan is an electrical engineer who has recently been made redundant. He has received a lump sum of £8,000. He plans to use the money to set up a business repairing washing machines and other domestic electrical appliances. The money will go towards buying tools and a second-hand van as well as a deposit on the rental for the premises and equipment for his workshop.

Ella has Level Three hairdressing qualifications and has worked for five years in a local salon. She now feels ready to set up her own business. She needs money to equip her new salon in rented property and set up initial advertising. She has worked hard on producing a good business plan and is confident that it shows that the business will be viable. She feels that it will take a couple of years for the business to become really profitable and wants to pay as little back as possible until then.

Tom wants to set up a business selling musical instruments. He has saved enough money to pay for start-up costs such as initial stock, advertising and fitting out the premises. However, he does not want to rent premises because he thinks that this is losing out on an investment opportunity. Ideally he would like to own the premises one day.

Ashraf runs a garage where he services and repairs customers' cars.
The business has been very profitable despite the fact that he is constantly having to chase customers to pay their bills.

He is thinking of offering MOT testing which would mean building an extension as well as installing specialist equipment.

Each of the businesses described above is operated by a sole trader who is looking for finance.

a) **On your own**, identify the most appropriate type(s) of finance to meet the needs of each business. Compare your ideas **with other members of your class**.

b) **Working in small groups**, consider each type of finance in turn and decide your answers to the following questions.

   i) Where would the money come from?

   ii) Would the amount have to be repaid at some stage?

   iii) Would any form of interest be charged?

   iv) What risks are involved to the person receiving the money?

ACTIVITY 2

COSTS AND BUDGETS

Some people struggle to keep to a budget, whereas others are very good at it. Businesses have no choice! If they continually spend more than they earn then they will have serious difficulties – as you will see in this section.

Task 1

Ben left university three years ago with a degree in business studies. He quickly found a job in a local authority planning department. For the first time in his life he had some money in his pocket – and he would be the first to admit that he has made the most of it. He has bought a new computer, a DVD player, expensive sound equipment and had holidays abroad. He also enjoys a good social life. He drives a seven-year-old car which his father bought him for his 21st birthday. He lives in rented accommodation where he has his own bedroom but shares other facilities.

Recently, however, he has noticed that some of his old classmates from university are buying flats or small houses. Damien, his best friend, is one of them. He tells Ben that he is silly spending money on rent when it could go towards paying off a mortgage. He calls the rent 'dead money'.

Income

Monthly salary after tax and insurance £1,500

Outgoings

Rent £250 a month

Gas, electricity and council tax £200 a month

Annual cost of car: insurance £1,000 and tax £110

Entertainment £100 a week

Petrol £150 per month

Food £70 per week

Season ticket for football club £420 per year

Monthly credit card repayment £150 (including £50 interest)

If buying a house

Potential mortgage £450 per month

Mortgage deposit required £5,000

Cost of buying flat/house (solicitor's fees etc) £1,500

As a result, Ben has decided to reappraise his finances to see what he can realistically achieve. He collects information from local estate agents and also visits some bank websites to get an idea of the cost of mortgages. He jots some figures down on a piece of paper.

Work in a group of two or three to carry out the following tasks:

a) Analyse Ben's expenditure list on the previous page and decide if you think he has missed anything out. One way to do this would be to think about your own spending over a week or month!

b) Amend Ben's list to take account of any omissions you have identified and include reasonable estimates for any items you include.

c) Ben aims to buy his own property in three years' time. He knows that he needs to save up his mortgage deposit and is planning to open a savings account. He thinks it would be a good idea to save enough each month so that when he has to pay a mortgage, instead of rent, he will not have to drastically adjust his expenditure pattern.

Prepare a financial plan (ie a budget) for him which would make sure that he can meet both these objectives.

d) Suggest how Ben could check the progress of his financial plans on a monthly basis.

e) Ben has heard that all costs can be fixed or variable, but doesn't know what this means. Write a brief explanation and identify which of his current outgoings are fixed and which are variable.

Task 2

Sarah has decided to start her own business and plans to open a coffee shop. She has found the ideal premises in a thriving city suburb and has asked for your help in planning her finances.

Work in groups of three or four to do this task.

a) Brainstorm the type of start-up costs that Sarah is likely to incur to set up this type of business.

b) Research the amount of money which would need to be allocated for each item on your list. You can use various sources to obtain realistic figures such as business rent levels from estate agents or your local paper, the cost of equipment and other items from suppliers' websites.

c) Decide whether Sarah should allow for a contingency amount to keep in reserve and be prepared to justify your decision.

d) Identify the total amount of money that you think Sarah will need to start her business and the sources of finance she could use.

Compare your ideas **as a class** and ask your tutor to judge which group would have given Sarah the best advice.

Task 3

Superdrive is an upmarket taxi firm owned and run by Mike Woolmer. It specialises in transporting business executives to and from airports. The business uses luxury cars and the drivers wear chauffeurs' uniforms. Until recently, the business has been quite profitable but is now only breaking even. Mike's accountant suggests that he should get a tighter grip on his expenses since the market is tight and increasing his prices is not an option. Acting on advice, Mike decides to produce a budget which forecasts expenditure.

The table below shows Mike's planned expenditure for a year (2007) followed by his actual expenditure. The budget itemises his expenditure and below the table are notes explaining some of the items.

Item	Planned for 2007 (£'000)	Actual for 2007 (£'000)	Variance (£'000)
Advertising	5	6	
Car hire	32	30	
Electricity	1	1	
Diesel	19	16	
Heating	2	1.5	
Miscellaneous	6	6	
Parking	4	5	
Telephone and Internet connection	1	1	
Premises	45	42	
Uniforms	5	4	
Valeting	7	6	
Wages	105	120	
Total			

Notes on the budget items:

- The business leases the cars it uses from a specialist firm. The deal includes a full repair and maintenance service. The cars are replaced every three years.
- The 'Miscellaneous' heading involves several small items of

expenditure, such as postage, stationery and so on.

- The 'Parking' item is included because Superdrive has to pay for parking at the airport while waiting for clients' flights to arrive.

- The business's premises include a secure parking compound with CCTV surveillance and a small office building used for administration.

- Superdrive supplies each driver with two uniforms and pays for these to be cleaned. The 'Uniform' heading includes replacement of worn-out garments.

- The 'Wages' item includes income tax and National Insurance payments made on behalf of the drivers.

Work on your own to complete the following tasks. Then compare your answers **as a class**.

a) Complete the table by calculating the variance and totals figures.

b) Look at the variance figures.

   i) Which should Mike be most concerned about? Give reasons for your choices.

   ii) What action do you think Mike should take as a result?

c) Even though some of the figures are under budget, Mike still wants to cut costs across the board. He decides to go for the highest four in terms of annual expenditure.

Identify these items and in each case suggest ways in which the figure could be reduced.

d) For the following items suggest where Mike obtained the 'actual' figure for expenditure: car hire, electricity, parking, uniforms and wages.

e) His accountant tells Mike that he has made a useful start in controlling his costs but says that it would be better if he worked out his planned and actual expenditure each month.

   i) Why do you think she has recommended Mike should do this every month?

   ii) Give the reasons why Mike needs to control his costs and his budget.

   iii) Explain, in as much detail as you can, the problems Mike could experience if he fails to monitor these.

Task 4

In July 2005 there was tremendous excitement when London was successful in its bid to run the 2012 Olympic Games. At the time, the cost of preparing for the games was budgeted at 2.4 billion pounds (£2.4 bn).

In March 2007 Tessa Jowell, the Government's Culture Secretary announced in the House of Commons that the figure had increased to £9.3 bn – almost four times the original figure.

London 2012 Olympic budget – March 2007

Spending the money	£	Raising the money	£
Olympic Delivery Authority:		Government (Treasury)	6 bn
Construction of site	3.1 bn	National Lottery	
Regeneration of		– originally	1.5 bn
Lower Lea Valley	1.7 bn	– top up amount	675 m
Tax bill	840 m	London mayor	925 m
Contingency fund	2.7 bn	London Development Agency	250 m
Extra security	600 m		
Elite athlete training and costs of			
Paralympics	390 m		

Actually staging the Games is a different issue. This is the responsibility of the London 2012 Organising Committee and the cost is currently estimated at £2 billion. This will be paid for by the sale of tickets as well as sponsorship, merchandising and selling broadcasting rights. The Organising Committee estimates that about 8 million tickets will be available for the Olympic Games and another 1.5 million for the Paralympics. The Committee is optimistic that sales will be around 90%. It has promised to price tickets fairly and thinks that more than 50% of tickets will cost less than £20. This will include free travel on London transport that day.

Apart from part a) below, do this task **in groups of three or four** and then compare your answers **as a class**.

a) **Test yourself!** Add up both columns of the budget (above) and see if they balance. Suggest reasons for any discrepancies you find.

b) **In small groups**, suggest the possible reasons for the huge change in the budget figure between 2005 and 2007.

c) Suggest the differences between budgeting for a business where trading has been taking place for several years and budgeting for a 'one-off' major project, such as the Olympic Games or the new Wembley Stadium.

   Which do you think is the more difficult to manage – and why?

d) In 2003, when the Olympic bid was first launched, the contingency fund stood at £1 billion.

   i) What is a 'contingency fund'?

   ii) Why is a contingency fund often included in a budget?

   iii) The government says this money will be 'locked away'. Can you suggest why?

   iv) Why do think the contingency fund has been increased?

e) Assuming that the average price of a ticket is £20 and that 90% are sold, calculate the contribution that ticket sales will make to the cost of staging the games.

f) Some news reports claim that the games will eventually cost £15 billion or more! Are they being realistic or scaremongering? Check out the official website at www.london2012.org (and news sites via Google) to find out if there have been any more increases to the budget for preparing the games since this activity was written.

ACTIVITY 3

FINANCIAL STATEMENTS

All businesses produce financial statements which summarise their performance over a particular period. Two of these are the profit and loss account and the balance sheet. You need to understand the purpose of the items in these statements and how they are calculated.

Task 1

Comfichair Ltd is a business which sells household furniture. It is located in a provincial town in the Midlands and has a reputation for selling quality products. The table below gives its summarised profit and loss figures for two years.

Working in groups of two or three, study the table carefully and then carry out the tasks that follow.

	2007 (£'000)	2008 (£'000)
Sales Income	10,200	9,700
Cost of Sales	6,500	6,500
Gross Profit	3,700	3,200
Operating Expenses	2,600	3,100
Operating Profit	1,100	100
Corporation Tax	300	30
Profit attributable to shareholders	800	
Dividend Payments	200	0
Retained Profit	600	70

a) Explain the purpose of a profit and loss account. In your explanation identify three groups of people or organisations who would be interested in the account, giving a reason in each case.

b) Sarah, a new member of staff at Comfichair, says she doesn't understand what the items mean.

Make notes for her that clearly explain what each entry in the left-hand column means. For income items, say where the money comes from. For expenditure, say what the money is spent on (for operating expenses, suggest at least five examples). For figures which are calculated, explain how this is done.

Be prepared to explain your notes verbally if you are asked to do so!

c) Your boss is a shareholder in Comfichair. Do you think he will be pleased with the performance of the business over the last two years? Give a reason for your answer which takes into account the following entries:

- The cost of sales for both years
- The amount of corporation tax paid in the second year
- The dividend payments
- The retained profits figures.

(Note: there is no need to use any financial ratios to answer this question).

d) List five types of records or documents that are needed to support the figures shown in the profit and loss account.

e) **In groups**, recommend the action that the managers at Comfichair should take over the next 12 months. Then compare your ideas **as a class**.

Task 2

Superlec Ltd is a family-owned retail business that sells domestic electrical goods, such as washing machines and televisions. In 2003 it had two retail outlets in separate towns and a warehouse. By 2007 it had sold the two shops and the warehouse and moved into a purpose-built combined shop and warehouse in a retail park on the outskirts of one of the towns. In addition, it sold its distribution fleet and leased the vehicles it needed. Superlec then changed its policy of selling only 'top-of-the-range' goods to lower-quality products and introduced an interest-free credit facility at the same time.

Compare the two sets of figures overleaf giving the balance sheets for the two years and then undertake the tasks which follow.

For simplicity, assume that there has been no inflation over the period.

Work in groups of two or three for this task.

a) Write your own definition of a balance sheet. Then identify the people who would, or could be interested in it and say why, in each case.

b) Write a brief definition of each item in the left-hand column.

c) Compare the figures for the two years and then answer the following questions:

i) How much extra value of land and buildings appear in the 2008 figures – and where did the extra money come from?

ii) In 2003, when the business owned its vehicles, these appeared as an asset in the balance sheet. Now that they lease them, where will these costs appear?

iii) Calculate the percentage increase in the 'Debtors' figure. What will the managers feel about this – especially given the new policy of interest-free credit?

    iv) What does the fall in the creditors figure suggest?

d) Explain what is meant by each of the following terms which are associated with balance sheets:

    i) Auditor's report

    ii) Intangible assets

    iii) Work-in-progress

    iv) Solvent/insolvent

    v) Capital

    vi) Bad debts

    vii) Depreciation

    viii) Companies House

Compare all your answers **as a class**.

	2003 (£'000)	2008 (£'000)
Fixed assets		
Land and buildings	3,000	4,000
Delivery vehicles	100	0
Total fixed assets	3,100	4,000
Current assets		
Stock	1,300	1,500
Debtors	320	570
Cash in bank	70	100
Total current assets	1,690	2,170
Current liabilities		
Creditors	500	400
Overdraft	100	0
Total current liabilities	600	400
Net current assets	1,090	1,770
Net total assets	4,190	5,770
Funded by		
Shares sold	2,000	3,000
Profit and loss account	2,190	2,770
Total	4,190	5,770

ACTIVITY 4

FINANCIAL RATIOS

Financial managers use accounting ratios to carry out a 'health check' on a company by assessing aspects such as its solvency and profitability. These can often provide a warning of possible future problems and provide useful guidance for both managers and potential investors.

Task 1

Work on your own to complete these tasks:

a) Match the name of each of the following financial ratios in the table with its correct formula.

Formulae:

A   Current assets − stock / Current liabilities
B   Net Operating profit / Total assets
C   Current assets / Current liabilities
D   Sales / Total net assets
E   Debtors x 365 / Sales
F   Net Operating profit / Sales
G   Gross profit / Sales
H   Sales / Stock

Type of ratio	Formula
Current ratio	
Acid test ratio	
Gross profit percentage	
Net profit percentage	
Return on capital employed	
Stock turnover	
Debtors' collection period	
Asset turnover	

b) For each ratio in the table above, explain what it says about the state of a business.

Check your answers with your tutor before attempting the next task.

Task 2

Work on your own for this task.

Table A (overleaf) gives financial information about two businesses – Alpha Ltd. and Beta Ltd.

a) Identify which items in Table A come from the balance sheet and which from the profit and loss account.

b) Use the information given in Table A to complete Table B.

Financial information about companies A and B for financial year 2007

Table A

Item	Alpha Ltd £'000	Beta Ltd £'000
Current assets	110	700
Current liabilities	70	600
Debtors	50	400
Gross profit	1,000	500
Net (or operating) profit	200	100
Sales	2,000	2,000
Stock	40	250
Total net assets	3,000	2,500

Table B

Item	Alpha Ltd ratios	Beta Ltd ratios
Current ratio		
Acid test ratio		
Gross profit percentage		
Net profit percentage		
Return on capital employed		
Stock turnover		
Debt collection period		
Asset turnover		

Compare and check your answers to Task 2 before starting Task 3.

Task 3

Work in groups of two or three for this task.

Your friend Alec is considering investing in either Business A or Business B and has asked for your advice.

a) For each business in turn, examine the completed Table B that you prepared in Task 2 and identify any figures that cause you concern.

b) Write comments on the difference between the two businesses for each of the following ratios:

i) Net profit percentage

ii) Return on capital employed

iii) Stock turnover

iv) Debt collection period

Remember when you do this that businesses can be successful by operating in different ways!

c) So that Alec understands what you have done, write an explanation for him on the value of accounting ratios for monitoring the financial state of a business.

d) What would you recommend Alec should do, and why?

Compare your answers **as a class**.

Task 4

To your surprise Alec is rather dismissive of your efforts! He argues that financial ratios are a waste of time because any business can manipulate its figures just to make them look good on a particular day.

You are horrified – but then wonder if he could be right! **As a group** investigate this issue and then hold a class debate.

One team should argue the benefits of financial ratios and the other should highlight their drawbacks. Both teams must produce evidence to support their claims.

Your tutor will decide which team has produced the more convincing argument.

UNIT 3 – INTRODUCTION TO MARKETING

This section focuses on grading criteria P1, P2; M1; and D1 from Unit 3 'Introduction to Marketing'.

Learning outcomes

1 Understand the concept and principles of marketing and their application in the business environment.

Content

1) **Understand the concept and principles of marketing and their application in the business environment**

Principles of marketing: overall concept; marketing definitions; principles; activities; marketing objectives (SMART); functions; the link between organisational objectives and marketing objectives; use of marketing principles, eg public, private and voluntary organisations, retail consumers, governments departments and agencies; planning, control and evaluation processes; development of e-marketing.

Marketing mix: 4 Ps (product, price, place, promotion).

Limitations and constraints on marketing: legal (consumer law, eg Sale of Goods Act 1979, Trade Descriptions Act 1968, Consumer Credit Act 1974; data protection, eg Data Protection Act 1998); voluntary constraints, eg Code of Advertising Practice and Advertising Standards Authority; pressure groups and consumerism; acceptable language.

Grading criteria

P1 describe the concept and principles of marketing

In addition to describing the overall concept of marketing, you will also need to describe each of the principles listed under 'Content' above.

P2 describe how the concept and principles are applied to the marketing of products in two organisations

It is sensible to identify two different, contrasting organisations that will enable you to apply the concept and principles to two different types of products (or services). Remember to state, too, how the limitations and constraints on marketing apply to your organisations.

M1 compare the effectiveness of the concepts and principles applied to the marketing of products by the two chosen organisations

This means that you will have to assess the extent to which the aims or goals of each marketing initiative or campaign have been achieved and give evidence to support your views. Again, you should include reference to the limitations and constraints on marketing.

D1 evaluate the concepts and principles applied to the marketing of products by a selected organisation and make recommendations for improvement

Here you are developing your answer to M1 by doing further research on one selected organisation, providing detailed analysis on its success in applying the concepts and principles of marketing to its products and, based on this evidence, making suggestions that will help it to be more successful in achieving its aims.

ACTIVITY 1

PRINCIPLES OF MARKETING

Many people confuse marketing with advertising. Do you? This section, which concentrates on the main concept of marketing and its key principles, should help you to recognise the difference!

Task 1

Carry out the first three parts of this task **on your own.**

Below are six definitions of marketing, but some of them are either inaccurate or incorrect.

a) Identify those that you think are correct and those that you think are not, and then justify your choice(s).

b) One is the official definition of marketing by the Chartered Institute of Marketing. Can you identify this?

c) Write your own definition, in which you sum up the basic concept of marketing in your own words. To help you, you may want to research additional (correct) definitions in books and on the Internet.

d) Compare your ideas **as a group**.

Definitions

A The management process responsible for identifying, anticipating and satisfying customer requirements profitably.

B Strategies used by businesses to promote their goods and provide good customer service.

C Producing, providing and promoting goods and services that the target market of customers want to buy.

D The methods used to identify, create and maintain profitable and satisfying relationships with customers.

E The management function which enables a business to identify and meet the needs of its actual and potential customers.

F Methods of advertising and selling goods and services positively and creatively.

Task 2

On the next page are three statements made by different businesses.

Read these statements and then work **in groups of two or three** to carry out the tasks below.

a) Identify which of the statements for each business is:

   i) The aim of the business

   ii) An organisational objective

   iii) A marketing objective.

b) All the businesses have different types of ownership. One is privately owned, one is in the public sector and the other is in the voluntary sector. Identify which is which and give a reason for each decision.

c) Identify which of the marketing objectives are SMART. Give a reason for your choice.

d) i) Suggest two marketing tactics each business could use to achieve its marketing objectives.

ii) Suggest two ways in which each business could evaluate the success of these tactics.

Business 1

To meet the health and social needs of local people.

To launch baby-massage classes in six new centres within 12 months.

To increase the range of mother-and-baby services in the area.

Business 2

To supply all major supermarkets.

To introduce our own range of healthy option, low calorie fruit drinks.

To be a leading specialist retailer of organic produce in the UK.

Business 3

To introduce a monthly lottery for supporters in June.

To provide prompt and appropriate information and support to people in need.

To increase funds from public donations by 5 %.

Task 3

Carry out the first three parts of this task **in groups of two or three.**

A college has decided to start a past students' association. The aim is to enable students to keep in touch with each other, and learn about new developments at the college, after they have left.

a) The marketing manager considers this initiative should be her department's responsibility. Do you think that she is correct? Give a reason for your opinion.

b) Investigate and identify four ways in which the college could utilise new technology and e-marketing to promote the association to students and past students.

c) The principal is prepared to allocate appropriate resources to this project provided that it is properly planned, monitored and controlled.

i) Identify TWO ways in which performance can be monitored.

ii) Explain what is meant by 'controlling' this type of project.

d) As a class, discuss and decide the key factors that would be likely to determine the success of this initiative, and how these should influence those responsible for planning and developing it.

ACTIVITY 2

THE MARKETING MIX

The marketing mix is often known as the '4 Ps'. It is the combination of activities that a business selects to best achieve its marketing objectives. Today many people refer to the '7 Ps', because these are more appropriate for businesses that provide a service – as you will see in this section.

Task 1

Carry out this task **in groups of two or three,** then compare your answers **as a class**.

a) Categorise each of the statements below by entering it in its correct quadrant in the basic marketing mix.

	Statement
A	Selling goods only online via the company website
B	Ensuring the distinctive brand logo is on all delivery vans, stationery and advertisements
C	Offering BOGOFF deals
D	Advertising on local radio
E	Offering cheap rates when business is slack
F	Offering 5-star facilities and service
G	Giving pensioners a 5% reduction
H	Having own warehouse and distribution network to ensure prompt, trackable deliveries
I	Producing books in hardback and paperback format
J	Employing specialist technical reps to visit business customers
K	Offering credit terms to business customers
J	Selling discontinued lines in a factory shop
L	Producing a variety of products, eg oil, unleaded petrol, leaded petrol and diesel fuel
M	Selling a service more cheaply to direct-debit customers

The marketing mix

Products	Price
Place	Promotion

b) The extended marketing mix consists of three more Ps, which specifically relate to service providers.

   i) Identify the names of these three additional Ps.

   ii) Categorise each of the following activities correctly, and enter them under the correct 'P', as you did for part **a)**:

	Statement
N	A customer service help desk
O	A play area for young children
P	Light and airy space with clear signs
Q	Clear customer complaints procedures
R	Self-service rapid check-outs
S	Distinctive uniforms for different staff
T	Personal account managers to deal with regular customers
U	Coffee shops and rest areas
V	The design of a website
W	'Contact us' link on a website with dedicated staff to respond

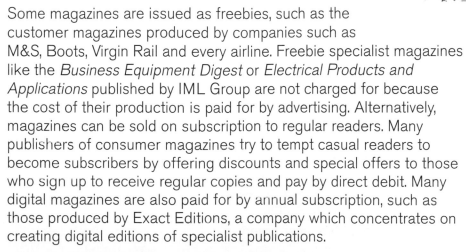

P............................

P...........................

P...........................

Task 2

According to the Periodical Publishers Association (PPA) the magazine market in the UK is worth £6.8 billion. It is divided into three sub-sectors:

- Business and professional magazines (value £3.3 billion)
- Consumer magazines (value £3 billion)
- Customer magazines (value £0.5 billion).

Even more importantly, the sector is growing. More magazines are published today than at any time in the past, mainly because new technology had enabled magazines to be produced more cheaply. They can also be distributed digitally rather than in print, with clickable adverts and email addresses for anyone who wants to find out more.

Some magazines are issued as freebies, such as the customer magazines produced by companies such as M&S, Boots, Virgin Rail and every airline. Freebie specialist magazines like the *Business Equipment Digest* or *Electrical Products and Applications* published by IML Group are not charged for because the cost of their production is paid for by advertising. Alternatively, magazines can be sold on subscription to regular readers. Many publishers of consumer magazines try to tempt casual readers to become subscribers by offering discounts and special offers to those who sign up to receive regular copies and pay by direct debit. Many digital magazines are also paid for by annual subscription, such as those produced by Exact Editions, a company which concentrates on creating digital editions of specialist publications.

Most magazines in Britain are still sold by retailers, with major supermarket chains having the edge on local newsagents in terms of volume of sales. Currently, the Office of Fair Trading is investigating newspaper and magazine distribution agreements. At present, publishers award wholesalers an exclusive territory in which they can distribute publications; the wholesaler cannot sell to any retailer outside this area. This means that no matter whether the wholesaler is reliable and efficient or not, a retailer cannot source supplies from anywhere else. This flies in the face of competition law in the UK, because the wholesaler is operating his own local monopoly and is protected from competitors. However, if the OFT changes the rules on distribution, this is likely to favour the supermarkets, which can use their power to drive through better deals with distributors. Whilst this will be in the interests of the customer, it will not favour small retailers nor the print media magazine producers.

In groups of two or three, carry out the following tasks:

a) Identify the difference between the three types of magazines listed at the start of the article, in terms of their target market.

b) Select one example of a magazine from each of the three sub-sectors. You will find ideas if you look at the PPA member list at www.ppa.co.uk/cgi-bin/go.pl/ppamembers/index.html. You can also investigate digital publications at www.exacteditions.com/.

c) For each magazine you have chosen, identify and chart its basic marketing mix in quadrants as you did in the first table for Task 1.

d) Identify any differences between the marketing mix for each product and suggest the reasons for these.

e) **As a class**, decide whether you think the OFT investigation is a good thing or not. Then look on its website at www.oft.gov.uk to find out if a decision has been made yet – and, if so, whether you agree with it!

Task 3

Allied to the marketing mix is the promotional mix. This relates to the range of promotional methods chosen to best attract the attention of the target market to a product.

Needless to say, the Periodical Publishers Association (PPA) concentrates on persuading businesses and their agencies that advertising in magazines is usually the most effective method of promoting a product or brand! To emphasise its point it provides several case studies. Some relate to consumer products or brands and others to B2B (business to business) promotions because the promotional mix that is most appropriate is usually different for an industrial or commercial product.

Its consumer brand case studies can be accessed at www.ppamarketing.net/. This is the PPA's own promotional site which provides information and advice on marketing. Its B2B case studies are available on www.bandpmedia.co.uk/ – another microsite which focuses on the needs of the business and professional magazine sector.

a) Access the PPA marketing site and choose a consumer brand case study which appeals to you.

i) Identify the methods which were used to promote the product in that campaign.

II) Identify the aims of the campaign and suggest why that particular promotional mix was selected.

b) Access the Business and Professional site and choose a B2B case study which appeals to you.

   i) Again, identify the promotional mix that was chosen.

   ii) Identify the aims of the campaign and suggest why those particular promotional methods were used.

c) **i)** Identify the differences between the methods used to promote both products in each of these types of markets.

   ii) Suggest other differences you are likely to find between the marketing mix for a consumer product and an industrial product.

d) Your college wants to promote its new courses. Some are for school leavers. Others are short courses which it wants to bring to the attention of local businesses. **As a class** discuss and decide your answers to each of the following questions:

   i) Suggest how the promotional mix will vary for each type of course.

   ii) Identify how other aspects of the marketing mix will also differ, and why.

   iii) Give examples of how each of the Ps in the extended marketing mix applies to colleges like yours.

Task 4

Product marketing is not an exact science, but key measures of success are usually increased sales and market share. Both have been the result of the marketing activities undertaken by Unilever to boost take-up of its Dove product range.

Dove started life in America as a 'cleansing bar' – or as a bar of soap to the British! Launched here in the 1990s, it is now part of an array of products, aligned more to the beauty counter than to the toiletry shelves. In 2001 antiperspirant/deodorant lines were added, followed by hair care products in 2001. In 2004 Dove introduced its 'Firming' range, followed by its body wash range in 2005. The latest addition is its 'Pro-Age' range, launched with the strapline 'because beauty has no age limit'.

Sales of all Dove products were boosted through its innovative 'real women' campaign. This proved hugely popular with women who identified and related to ordinary women of all shapes and sizes in the advertisements, rather than air-brushed, size zero models! Dove has since launched its 'real beauty' campaign in conjunction with ASDA, as well as a self-esteem fund to help young girls with body image issues. In 2007 it carried out a big online survey to find out what women are currently thinking at www.dove.co.uk – its UK microsite.

Work in groups of two or three for this task.

a) Check that you understand the main concept and principles of marketing by researching these online and in any textbook you are using.

b) Find out more about Dove, its products and campaigns online. There are a number of microsites featuring Dove as well as relevant information on the main Unilever site. You will find these easily using any good search engine. Read the press releases related to the Dove campaign as well as product information. You can also find out more on the PPA website where Dove features as one of its case studies. Dove also won the PPA Marketing's consumer Magazine Advertiser of the Year award in 2005.

c) Identify the main aspects of Dove's marketing mix. As you do this, decide the key factors which have influenced the management decisions relating to each major aspect of the mix (ie each of the four Ps).

d) Identify how the marketing team at Dove has applied the concept and principles of marketing to boost sales of the product.

e) How effective do you think their efforts have been? Give a reason for your answer.

ACTIVITY 3

LIMITATIONS AND CONSTRAINTS ON MARKETING

Most people are aware that it is illegal to lie about a product to make a sale and that a grossly offensive advertisement would not be acceptable – even if they are not too sure about the finer points! You need to know rather more. In addition, you also need to think about the activities of pressure groups who may take matters into their own hands to influence marketing activities!

Task 1

Carry out the following task **on your own**:

a) Decide whether each of the actions in the table opposite is illegal, unethical, or neither.

b) For any activity that you decide is illegal, identify the law that is being broken.

c) For any activity that you decide is unethical, decide whether the business would be prevented from doing it and if so, by whom.

Then compare your answers **with other members of your class**.

Task 2

The advertising laws in the UK are changing with a new piece of legislation – The Unfair Commercial Practices Directive (UCPD). Broadly, this will mean that consumer practices that are considered to be unfair or misleading will be illegal. As a result, the UK Government will need to repeal or amend some of its current consumer legislation.

The Directive must come into force on 12 December 2007 – so if you are reading this activity after that date it is already law.

In groups of three or four:

a) Check the content of the UCPD and its guidance to businesses on the DTI website at www.dti.gov.uk/consumers/buying-selling/ucp/index.html

b) Check whether your answers to Task 1 took account of this new piece of legislation!

	Activity	Your decision
A	Promising to deliver a product by an unachievable deadline date to make the sale	
B	Leaving slightly damaged goods on sale in the hope customers won't notice the defects	
C	Exaggerating the features of a product and misleading the buyer as to its suitability	
D	Telling a sob story to a customer to make a sale	
E	Sharing a customer's confidential data with another business in exchange for similar information	
F	Adding anyone who emails you to your customer database and sending them regular email newsletters	
G	Claiming goods are at a new, marked down price, when they are not	
H	Promoting items with the highest margins to customers to maximise commission and profits	
I	Using size zero models in a clothes advert	
J	Attracting customers by advertising bargain goods when only a few exist and then selling more expensive substitutes	
K	Refusing to give a customer a refund for a faulty purchase	
L	Exaggerating the health benefits of a cereal in an advert	
M	Placing children's varieties on low shelves so that children will spot them easily and pester their parents to buy them	
N	Pointing out the weaknesses of a competitor's product in an advert	

Task 3

Derek has always loved working with wood. Ten years ago he started his own business making custom-designed rocking horses and wheeled toys for young children under four. They have been so successful that he now employs 15 people to help him to fulfil the orders he receives from toy stores around Britain.

Derek's son and daughter, Alex and Stephanie, now both work in the business and are very keen on expanding it. Stephanie feels they would do better to sell direct to customers, especially online, as this would mean they could expand their market. Alex argues that they can also increase demand substantially by advertising their products so that children will see them and start to pester their parents to buy one. He also wants to do something spectacular involving young children to get free coverage in magazine and newspaper articles. He wants their toys to become as popular as the well-known wheely-bugs that took the market by storm in 2006.

Derek is not so sure. He is concerned that they could fall foul of many laws and regulations if they just go ahead without any thought or research – and has asked for your help. He is a member of the British Toy and Hobby Association and suggests you start there, and by looking at the Advertising Standards Authority website.

Carry out the following tasks **in groups of three or four**.

a) Research the toy market and the limitations and constraints on marketing that apply to it.

b) Prepare a short (10-minute) presentation in which you:

   i) Summarise the main constraints that apply to marketing in the toy industry.

   ii) Identify the main issues that relate to Stephanie's plans.

   iii) Identify the main issues that relate to Alex's plans.

   iv) Propose an appropriate way forward for the business.

Task 4

As a nation we spent £134 billion in UK supermarkets in 2006 – with the lion's share going to the four largest: Tesco, ASDA, Sainsbury and Morrisons.

Whilst all these businesses are profitable and have increasing sales, not all of them are growing at the same rate. The outstanding winner has been Tesco, with 31% market share and year-on-year record profits. In 2006 these amounted to £2.2 billion.

Morrisons, in contrast, has experienced a few problems, particularly after it bought Safeway in 2004. In 2005 it issued several profit warnings. Although matters improved in 2006, the situation was still worrying. The business has 11% market share and needs to increase this figure. As a result, in March 2007, its Chief Executive Marc Boland announced Morrisons' plans to reposition itself. It will replace its 'more reasons to shop at Morrisons' slogan and move away from its 'value for money/low price' image. It intends to open smaller stores and to revamp its website — possibly as a precursor to selling online. In the future it may even join its competitors by selling non-food merchandise in its stores.

Change is seen as particularly important since Morrisons expanded south from its roots in northern England. It now needs to attract a wider range of customers — hence its new focus on freshness, clear packaging and good service.

Moving south hasn't been the only problem Morrisons has had to face. As part of its Oceans campaign, Greenpeace targeted the business as Britain's worst seafood retailer in 2006. But there again, Greenpeace also campaigned against ASDA and Tesco, too!

Tesco is no stranger to pressure groups. Its plans to build a store in Harrogate, North Yorkshire, split the community — 52% wanted HG to remain the only postcode area on the British mainland without a Tesco store. Tesco's continued growth has long been a target, both of the press and of Tescopoly, which paints horror scenarios of a world eventually owned and controlled by Tesco. But the little people can have an effect too. When 1,000 residents of a 'dry' community in Bourneville protested against Tesco's application to sell alcohol at its proposed Express store, Birmingham City Council licensing sub-committee turned down the application.

Working in groups of two or three:

a) Start by investigating Morrisons to prepare a summary that describes how the organisation has applied the concept and principles of marketing to its stores in the past. Do this by carrying out the following activities:

   i) Find out more about Morrisons by checking out its website at www.morrisons.co.uk. In particular, check the investors and press releases section to find out about its current plans and performance. You can also obtain useful background information on the Wikipedia website as well as on the BBC news website.

   ii) Identify and plot the traditional marketing mix for Morrisons. As you do this, consider the factors that have influenced the elements in this mix.

   iii) Identify any constraints that should influence Morrison's future marketing activities. This should include the actions of pressure groups.

   iv) Prepare your summary, based on the information you have obtained during your investigations.

b) Carry out the same activities, but this time for Tesco.

   i) Research this organisation and check its current plans and performance. Find out, too, about the marketing strategies it has used to become so successful.

   ii) Identify and plot the marketing mix for Tesco. Again you need to consider the influences that have determined this.

   iii) Investigate Tescopoly at www.tescopoly.org. Then check out other negative reports in the press and other constraints on its activities. Consider whether — or how — Tesco should respond to these.

iv) Decide how Tesco has applied the concept and principles of marketing to its business.

c) Compare the effectiveness of both supermarkets in applying the concepts and principles to marketing their businesses. When you do this, identify any important differences between the two approaches.

d) Evaluate the way in which Morrisons has applied the concepts and principles of marketing to its business and make recommendations for improvement based on your investigations.

e) Present your findings to your class in the form of a short presentation.

This section focuses on grading criteria P3, P4, P5; M2, M3; and D2 from Unit 4 'Effective People, Communication and Information'.

Learning outcomes

2 Know how to communicate using appropriate methods.

3 Understand different types of information and how it can be processed.

4 Be able to present information effectively.

Content

2) Know how to communicate using appropriate methods

Audience requirements: eg age, gender, ethnicity, special needs; readability, legibility; attention span, accessibility, interest, distraction avoidance; business experience and knowledge, industry-related experience and knowledge

Methods of written communication: eg letter, memorandum, fax, invoice; flow charts, publicity material, email and screen based; SMS (short message service), www (worldwide web)

Methods of non-written communication: telephone call, video conferencing

Technologies: computers, touch screens, digital broadcasting; DVD (digital versatile/ video disc); mobile phones; the Internet and WAP (wireless application protocol).

3) Understand different types of information and how it can be processed

Types of information: verbal; written; on-screen; multimedia; web-based

Features of information: internal; external; primary; secondary; current nature of information; life expectancy of information

Purpose of information: updating knowledge; informing future developments; offering competitive insight; communicating sales promotions; inviting support for activities

Information gathering: information sources, eg the worldwide web, using search engines, business communications, government statistical sources, news sources

Adherence to legislation: eg copyright and related legislation, designs and patents, intellectual copyright, w3w (World Wide Web Window), disability discrimination, equal opportunities.

4) Be able to present information effectively

Presentation methods to meet the needs of the user: eg document, use of style, verbal presentations, role plays, on-screen multimedia presentation, use of images, web-based presentation, mutilingual support

Output requirement: eg resolution of images, page layout, text formatting, use of tables, combining information from a range of applications, use of specialist software and hardware.

GRADING CRITERIA

P3 outline electronic and non-electronic methods for communicating business information using examples for different types of audience

This means listing or itemising different types of communication methods, both written and electronic, and identifying which methods are suitable for different recipients and different messages. You could choose to do this in a table.

P4 select information from three sources and manipulate it, adhering to legislation, for business purposes

Manipulating information means changing it to make it suitable for particular recipients. You will need to identify appropriate information and then alter it – such as putting numerical information into a chart or graph or selecting and entering numbers into a spreadsheet to make calculations.

P5 present the information from P4 using three different methods

Remember that you can use ICT effectively to help you achieve this criterion.

M2 justify the reasons for using different methods for communicating business information

This means explaining why you have chosen particular methods, with reference to the specific needs of recipients.

M3 demonstrate and justify the use of suitable presentation methods using information from three sources

This means making a presentation in which you show the methods you have chosen to use and give your reasons.

D2 assess the suitability of the three methods used for communicating and presenting information

This means you identify the strengths and weaknesses of each method and explain these, bearing in mind the needs of your target audience and the type of information you are communicating in each case.

ACTIVITY 1

COMMUNICATING INFORMATION USING APPROPRIATE METHODS

Effectively communicating does not just mean writing documents precisely and grammatically or having the ability to speak clearly – although both of these are important in business. It also means being able to select the correct method of communicating to meet the needs of the audience. You need to understand the difference between the various electronic and non-electronic methods available and the circumstances in which each of these would be most suitable.

Task 1

Meeting the needs of an audience means taking account of their particular requirements – and this means understanding who your customers are and what they want. For example, Hasbro, makers of board games Monopoly and Scrabble introduced Express versions which can be completed much more quickly, because it found that today's children, who are more used to texting than playing board games, have a shorter attention span than their parents. As another example, books written by famous authors such as Jacqueline Wilson and JK Rowling are available not just in standard print versions but also in large print, unabridged audio, Braille and as Daisy Talking Books for young readers with special needs.

The same applies to communications. You can only communicate appropriately if you know the requirements of your audience and how to meet these, as you will see in this task, which tests your skill at identifying the needs of diverse audiences. You must then suggest how these would affect the way in which any promotional communications should be prepared.

Carry out this task **in groups of two or three.**

You work for a marketing and communications agency that produces publicity and informational material for its clients. Part of the job of the agency is to identify which media to use, both electronic and non-electronic, to communicate with a target audience.

a) With the agreement of your tutor, select ONE of the businesses or products below as your client:

- A vehicle recovery service
- An environmentally friendly car
- A new television 'soap' docudrama
- A national cinema chain
- An energy-saving heating system
- A new digital camera
- A chain of city hotels in the UK
- A luxury executive jet service.

b) Identify the target audience with whom you would be communicating and then identify its main requirements. Some factors to consider are given in column one of the table below, but you may think of others to add. Equally, not all these factors may

Different audience requirements	Applicable/non-applicable	Affect on style/content of materials	Affect on methods of communication
Age			
Gender			
Ethnicity			
Special needs			
Readability			
Legibility			
Attention span			
Accessibility			
Interest			
Distraction avoidance			
Business experience and knowledge			
Industry-related experience and knowledge			

apply to your business or product. Then decide how this would affect the materials produced and the way in which you would communicate the information.

Note: try to avoid stereotyping different groups as you do this task!

c) Produce a proposal for your client in which you give your recommendations for communicating with different sectors of its target audience. Remember, you must justify (ie give reasons for) every recommendation that you make.

d) Give your proposal in a short presentation which involves every member of the group. Remember to take account of the needs of your audience when you do this!

Task 2

People in business need to communicate with other people on many occasions. For each of the situations below, identify the method you consider would be the most appropriate to use and then give a reason for your choice.

	Method chosen	Reason(s)
To send a copy of a spreadsheet to your boss, for approval		
To remind a regular client of an appointment time		
To confirm a meeting with a group of staff		
To respond to a customer's complaint		
To illustrate the complaints procedure and explain to customers or clients how it operates		
To discuss sales strategies with two colleagues who are about to visit an overseas client		
To provide regularly updated FAQs information to customers		
To query the new tax code you have been given		
To report the outcome of an investigation into computer misuse in the department to your MD		
To provide details of a transaction and the amount owed to a customer with a visual impairment		
To allow visitors to find their own way around a large complex		
To enable customers to see a videoed presentation about the firm's products		

Task 3

The traditional way of highlighting an issue or putting pressure on politicians is to write a letter to the press, your MP, or both. But when Stop Climate Chaos (SCC), a coalition of more than 50 UK organisations, decided to mobilise public opinion in the UK, it chose a different method. In October 2006 it launched its iCount campaign.

New visitors to its website at www.icount.org.uk are invited to sign up and, with a few clicks of their mouse, email the Prime Minister. They are encouraged to take specific actions to save CO_2, including buying the iCount pocket book: *Your Step-by-Step Guide to Climate Bliss*. Each action they take is logged and each new member adds one more to the iCount online ticker – currently standing at 39,259 people. New members are encouraged to spread the word by emailing their friends, who can also join by texting iCount to 84424.

In addition to items like news releases and a list of coalition members on the iCount website there are also details of events and other ways to get involved. In November 2006, more than 25,000 people went to Trafalgar Square to hear Razorlight, K T Tunstall and Miranda Richardson, amongst others, demand that politicians take more action to reduce UK carbon emissions.

Once you have read the article above, answer the following questions **in groups of two or three.**

a) In-depth information about Stop Climate Chaos is available on the main website at www.stopclimatechaos.org. This includes detailed facts and figures on climate change. Suggest why this information has not been included on the iCount website.

b) Check out both websites. For each one, identify the target audience and its main requirements. Then explain how well you think these needs have been met and justify your opinion.

c) Identify the ways in which Stop Climate Chaos has utilised technology to help to achieve its communication objectives.

d) All charities and pressure groups need to appeal to a wide audience for funding and support. They also need to communicate different messages, such as when they want to raise public awareness, raise more money or explain how they have used their money. Select a large national charity of your choice and then, through its website, list the main methods by which it communicates with its audience. For each method, suggest why this has been chosen.

e) Compare the methods used by your charity with those used by iCount. Suggest the reason for any differences you find.

Task 4

On your own, collect six different examples of written business communications.

a) For each one, identify why this method has been used, bearing in mind its message and the requirements of the target audience.

b) **As a class**, compare your examples and group them under different types of communications. Then decide which are the most effective in each category – and why.

ACTIVITY 2

UNDERSTANDING AND PROCESSING DIFFERENT TYPES OF INFORMATION

We are surrounded by information every day. Some may be detailed, important or urgent and need to be written down. Some may have been researched or produced for a specific purpose. There may be legal implications for the way information is gathered or used. Understanding about different types of information and how they can be processed is essential to communicating effectively, and is the focus of this section.

Task 1

Test your own ability to communicate clearly with this task!

You work for a small business which imports many goods from Europe. It has recently taken delivery of a consignment of infrared health lamps to sell to chemist shops and health stores. When these were unpacked, your boss discovered that the user instructions on the leaflet are in German.

To solve the problem, she entered the information into Google for a translation. The result was understandable – but only just! As a result she has asked you to rewrite the instructions, so that they make sense to English-speaking buyers.

Carry out this task **on your own,** and then compare your finished results **as a class**.

Instructions

Infrared lamp

General one of references

This infrared lamp are effectively in the short-wave infrared range and therefore for the heat irradiation particularly well suitable.

The infrared emitter delivers immediately after switching on the full thermal output.

In order to obtain an optimal radiant heat, you keep please a distance (skin surface to emitters) from at least 50 cm.

Irradiation with the infrared lamp can arbitrarily often be repeated.

However those should amount to having between the irradiation several hours.

One irradiation duration of approx. 15 minutes is in most cases sufficient.

Avoid after the irradiation a too high temperature waste.

With serious pain conditions, inflammations and symptoms of unsettled origin only consult the physician.

Infrared lamp in bathing, shower or other humid rooms do not use!

Repairs at electrical items, including exchange of the inlet, may be accomplished only by specialists.

Task 2

To your surprise, your grandfather has just announced that he is thinking of buying an iPod. He is very keen on sport and current affairs and likes the idea of listening to podcasts on cricket, football and news bulletins when he is out or in the garden, rather than sitting at his computer. He also likes the idea of storing music files, as he's very keen on jazz and an ardent fan of Katie Melua! At present he has a laptop with Windows XP and a broadband connection that your father sorted out for him some time ago.

Your grandfather is the first to admit that he hasn't the faintest idea about which type of iPod would be best. He has tried reading up about storage capacity and says that he is fed up of terms like 'DRM', 'AAC', 'MP3' 'kbps' and 'gig this and gig that' which he doesn't understand. He has heard of iTunes but doesn't know how it works and he read in the papers that tracks are now sold at two different prices, based on whether or not they have copy protection, but this has confused him even more. From what he is saying, you don't think he even realises that he can rip tracks from the CDs he already owns onto the iPod. He's also worried that he won't 'get on with' wearing headphones – and was surprised when you said he could listen using speakers instead.

As a favour, you have said you will research this whole issue for him and send him the information he needs attached to an email.

Do this by carrying out the following tasks **on your own**:

a) Research and prepare a comparative table which identifies the different iPod models that are available, the storage options and prices. Include for each model the main features that would be useful for your grandfather.

b) Write a brief description of how iTunes operates and how the issue of copy protection currently applies to music files.

c) Identify accessories your grandfather may wish to buy as well as sites where he could obtain the podcasts he wants. Note down any relevant price information.

d) Prepare a brief glossary that gives the meaning of all the specialist terms you have used or which your grandfather might read.

e) Write a short paragraph which summarises what iPods can do, what type of files can be stored on them, the benefits (and any drawbacks) of using them.

f) Put all the information prepared for **a)** to **e)** in the best order on an information sheet to attach to the email.

g) Write an accompanying email message. You are rather worried that your grandfather might put the information to one side for six months and then expect it still to be valid! For that reason, include a note about how long it is likely to remain accurate.

Task 3

Jill Burns started her own website business, Holidaylowdown, as a hobby five years ago. This asks people who have been on holiday to provide honest feedback on their experiences. The website has been quite successful with some large tour operators paying to advertise on the site. However, they are only interested in websites with a large number of visitors and with many users providing information. Jill tracks her visitors and knows that numbers have been falling recently, probably because of the increase in competitive sites offering a similar service.

Jill thinks the site needs a revamp. In addition, she is aware that she has never given much consideration to accessibility – even though this is a key requirement of the Disability Discrimination Act. She recently read that the UN has passed a Convention on the Rights of Persons with Disabilities which includes a requirement that the Internet must be made accessible. Moreover, she also read that there are 10 million disabled people in the UK who spend around £80 billion a year. She realises that focusing on this area, and inviting people with disabilities to comment on aspects of travel could give her business a USP to differentiate it from her competitors.

Jill has asked for your help to obtain the information for her and has suggested various sources. She doesn't want any in-depth technical information as she will pay an expert to redesign the site. She does, however, want to know more about the whole topic before she does this.

Carry out this task **in groups of two or three**. Agree with your tutor whether each group should carry out each part of the task, or whether you should allocate these between the class.

Obtain the information required and then prepare to present it back verbally to the rest of the class. This means that the information needs to be in a logical order and kept simple.

- Information on competitive websites to Jill's, focusing on how they are set out and the factors that are most appealing.
- Information on the Web content Accessibility Guidelines at www.w3.org/WAI. Jill doesn't want technical details but is more interested in the business case for accessibility.
- Information on the RNIB's See it Right initiative and logo at www.rnib.org.uk/wac and the benefits for organisations and users.
- Information about web access for disabled users at www.abilitynet.org.uk/web.
- Information on the growth of online advertising in the UK, using any online sources of your own choice.
- A comparison of some of Jill's competitive websites with some sites known for their accessibility, such as www.gateway2at.org, www.homeoffice.gov.uk, www.landg.com, www.ukschoolgames. com/. (Checking on 'accessibility' where this is an option on the sites will help you to identify key features).

Task 4

Intellectual property issues are constantly in the press. From fake designer handbags and pirate software to illegal music and movie downloads which are copied and sold at car boot sales, the Internet has put the whole argument centre-stage.

A recent case centres on YouTube, the video-sharing website owned by Google. Twentieth Century Fox angrily demanded the name of an American user who posted episodes of *24* and *The Simpsons* on the site. Viacom launched a $1 billion lawsuit against Google for copyright infringement over *SpongeBob*. Parents have now been warned to be careful what their offspring upload on the site – even using a pop song as a backing track is unlawful.

Legally, Google has only to comply with a request for items to be removed when they are identified. This infuriates firms like Viacom who argue it has the technology to monitor YouTube more proactively.

Some people argue that Twentieth Century Fox and Viacom should get real. YouTube only shows clips – which are good adverts for the products. They argue it is more sensible for businesses like Viacom and Google to work together to find a solution, otherwise the only winners are the lawyers.

Should movie clips be immune from IP law? And what about movie downloads? Should ISPs be forced to close down sites that offer free downloads?

Debate this issue **as a class.**

One team should take the view that businesses must learn to adapt and work together to cope with the Internet – as EMI did when it agreed to remove copyright restrictions on its music files. They could suggest innovative ways in which businesses could cope with people wanting to download movie files which could perhaps put the pirates out of business!

The other team should take the view that any type of piracy harms the activities of legitimate businesses, hits their profits and promotes the distribution of illegal products. They could argue that legislation is the best way of dealing with this and should be strengthened.

Sites to help you in your research include www.ipo.gov.uk/ipportal.htm www.thetrucosts.org, www.respectcopyrights.org, www.stopfakes.gov, www.musicunited.org, www.keepthemusicalive.com and www.copyrightkids.org. You could also usefully research this issue on any news sites, especially to find out the latest situation about movie downloads and clampdowns on car boot sales by Trading Standards Officers.

ACTIVITY 3

PRESENTING INFORMATION EFFECTIVELY

Good presentation can make the difference between information that is clear and easy to understand – and that which is not. It needs to be user-friendly and fit for purpose. This means understanding which methods best meet the needs of the users as well as how to obtain good quality output. This section will enable you to practise your skills.

Task 1

According to money education charity Credit Action, personal debt in Britain increases by £1 million every 4 minutes and stood at £1,310 billion at the end of February 2007. Some of this debt is planned and manageable – but much of it isn't – which is why every day over 5,000 people seek advice on debt problems from the Citizens Advice Bureau. Some people become desperate as they find themselves in a vicious circle of juggling their commitments to meet minimum interest payments, never managing to repay the principal sum they borrowed. As a result, in 2007, the major banks wrote off £6.64 billion of debts they had made to private individuals during 2006.

This problem is not just confined to adults. According to a study by pfeg (Personal Finance Education Group), over half of England's teenagers have been or are in debt by the time they are 17 and 66% think about money every day. 90% worry about their money and spending but think that overdrafts and credit cards are methods they can use to help them. 23% believe that having an overdraft allows you to spend more than you earn every month and one in 20 teenagers didn't know that they had to pay back money they spent using a credit card.

pfeg is an education charity which wants to ensure youngsters today don't make their own lives miserable because of their lack of financial skills. It wants to equip school leavers with the confidence, skills and knowledge they need in financial matters to take part fully in society. In 2006 it launched its Learning Money Matters initiative to give 1.8 million pupils the opportunities to receive financial education. The charity works with teachers, government, consumer bodies and financial industry representatives to provide high-quality advice, support and resources to secondary schools and teachers.

Read the article above and then carry out the following tasks **in groups of two or three**.

a) You also work for a voluntary organisation that works with a variety of stakeholders. Your boss has heard that the pfeg website could provide a helpful example because of the way it is designed. He has asked you to go to http://www.pfeg.org/, assess key aspects of the site and write your findings in an appropriate document. The layout and design is up to you. Your investigations should include:

   i) Identification of the way in which the charity has divided its site into different 'audience' groups and your explanation of the reasoning for this.

   ii) Practical examples of how the type of information and its presentation differs for the various user groups. In each case, suggest why these formats have been used.

iii) Identification of how the charity has differentiated between the information produced and presented for different age groups and has also met the need for cultural diversity.

iv) An assessment of the website's accessibility for different users.

v) An evaluation of the benefits and drawbacks of using video testimonies on the Learning Money Matters microsite.

vi) An assessment of the layout of its Newsletters and Annual Reports, particularly the way the financial information is presented.

b) Your sister works in a primary school teaching 10-year-olds.

i) Using the pfeg site for guidance, prepare a poster for her pupils to illustrate one or two key principles about money management that are relevant to that age group. The layout and design are entirely up to you, but you should include some 'numbers' to illustrate your theme.

ii) Write a brief role play that the pupils could carry out, to emphasise the key points.

Task 2

In 2007 the Home Office announced the extension of 'talking' CCTV cameras to a number of areas across Britain. First introduced in Middlesbrough in 2003, these cameras have loudspeakers attached so that miscreants can be scolded, warned or given advice to encourage them to behave.

The Home Office proposed to start by using local children to record the information, with school competitions to identify the child with the most suitable voice in each area.

Will this method of presentation be effective? And what should the information in the 'messages' be?

a) In small groups, identify five types of anti-social behaviour that could be spotted by CCTV cameras. For each one, prepare a message that you think would be effective.

b) Role-play these to the rest of the class and vote for the ones you think are most effective.

c) As a class, debate whether this method of presenting information to prevent crime is likely to be effective or not. Give reasons for your opinions and your views. For example, you may think it would be better backed up by other methods (eg a poster campaign) or you may think there is no real role for communications in preventing crime.

Task 3

Jake and Jessica are vets who run the Old Barn Veterinary Centre. For several years they have produced and posted a quarterly newsletter to their regular clients. The newsletter is printed in black and white and is mainly text-based although Jake has occasionally included clipart pictures of animals to liven it up a bit.

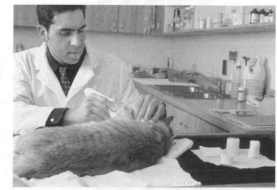

The practice is expanding rapidly and last month it appointed a new practice manager, Helen. Helen has recommended that they stop posting out the newsletter and instead launch their own website. This will provide information about the practice and the staff. The newsletters, she says, could be put on the website and downloaded by clients either as pdf or HTML files. It would be a simple matter to include photos of animals that have been treated in the practice.

Jake isn't too sure that this will meet the requirements of all their clients. Jessica is concerned that their very basic newsletters will look drab and is worried about the implications of putting pictures of animals they treat online.

You have been asked to advise them and produce a report giving your findings and recommendations. You will then summarise this verbally for Jake, Jessica and Helen in a short presentation.

Work **in small groups of two or three** to carry out this task.

a) Research some websites of veterinary practices in England and Wales and identify the main types of information they contain.

b) Research examples of newsletters online and note down key features of their design and layout.

c) List the main differences between the layout and design of a webpage and those of a printed page.

d) Research the type of specialist software that the Centre may need to buy to optimise the creation of its new website and the presentation of information.

e) Identify the advantages and drawbacks of including photographs of animals and video clips on the website. Note, too, any legal issues surrounding these.

f) Identify two or three types of information that the Centre could include as tables, to break up the text.

g) Prepare your report making sure that you identify clearly how the Centre should communicate the information online and giving reasons for your decisions.

h) Prepare a short presentation during which you summarise the key findings and recommendations in your report.

Task 4

You work for Farmhouse Fare – a medium-sized food production company which focuses on healthy and organic products. Your boss, Karen Harding, has read the article below and has used it as the basis for producing a new healthier pizza range.

The pizzas will have low salt and fat levels and be made using fresh organic vegetables. Karen wants to use this information to promote the pizzas to all her major buyers. These include several schools and colleges in the area, as well as a leading supermarket chain.

At the annual meeting of the American Chemical Society in Chicago, food researchers at the University of Maryland claimed to have discovered the secret of healthier pizzas. The secret lies in increasing the number of antioxidants in the pizza base. This is done by increasing the baking temperature to 285 degrees centigrade – from the normal 200 degrees – which results in a surge in antioxidants up to 82%. Baking the base for longer – 14 minutes – causes an additional increase of 60%. Leaving the pizza base to ferment for two days before baking also boosts the antioxidants by up to 100%. For the best results the pizza base should be made with whole-wheat flour, which contains more antioxidants than refined flour.

(Adapted from article in Guardian newspaper, 27 March 2007)

Karen is aware that pizzas can never be classed as healthy food, but is a realist. She thinks that as pizzas will always be a popular choice then the answer is to make them as healthy as possible. She therefore wants her sales promotion to include relevant information on aspects of a healthy diet – particularly for young people – such as that propounded by the Government and the British Dietetic Association. She thinks it would also be useful to include some current facts and figures – probably as a table – relevant to weight and diet in the UK.

Your task is to work **in a group of three or four** to do the following:

a) Identify and research the type of information that Karen could use with the help of an appropriate search engine. Find out, too, the latest information relating to healthy eating guidelines and weight issues in the UK by using government statistical sources and relevant news sources.

b) Decide on an appropriate name for the pizza range which will help to reflect its healthy image.

c) Identify the best information to include in the promotion and the order in which it should appear.

d) Write a brief opening paragraph to communicate the key message to readers. Be careful not to make any claims relating to healthy eating that could be challenged!

e) Karen cannot decide whether to produce this information as a leaflet or a sales letter. In addition she is also considering launching a microsite to promote the pizzas, perhaps including a multimedia presentation.

   i) Mock up a leaflet so that Karen can see what it would look like. Include relevant illustrations and tables at appropriate points.

   ii) Produce a sales letter which Karen could send out instead, which contains the key information.

iii) Create a brief presentation which summarises the way the pizzas are made and the benefits of this method.

f) **In your groups**, assess the suitability of each of the three methods with reasons for your choice.

g) Present all your ideas to the rest of your class, including your assessment of which method would be best to use to communicate with Karen's buyers.

h) When each team has presented, vote on the best one. Then, **as a class**, suggest why this one was the most effective.

ASSESSED ASSIGNMENTS

UNIT 38 – Understanding Business Ethics

This section contains a sample assignment for Unit 38, Understanding Business Ethics. The assignment covers Pass, Merit and Distinction criteria and requires evidence of substantial research by learners, particularly to meet the Distinction criterion. You will read learner answers at each level as well as tutor feedback to each of these.

Read these answers yourself and try to identify both good and weak points *before* you read the tutor feedback. Then check if you were right. Use this information to identify the common pitfalls and errors that learners often make. In some cases this can mean having to rewrite and resubmit work, sometimes several times, to achieve specific grading criteria. You can avoid this by learning from the mistakes

highlighted and by taking note of the good practice demonstrated in the good answers.

Remember that this section is just as valuable whether you are studying Unit 38 yourself or not! This is because many of your assessments for a BTEC National qualification in Business will involve written assignments and you will often be expected to research information when you are preparing your answers. Doing this effectively, writing clearly and concisely, preparing the work in the correct format and answering the question(s) properly are all vital skills you need to demonstrate. Getting this right early in your course will save you valuable time, help to build your confidence and enable you to gain the best grades possible from the start.

SAMPLE ASSIGNMENT

Unit title: Understanding business ethics

Unit 38, Assignment 38.1

ABOUT THIS ASSIGNMENT

This assignment requires you to apply the knowledge and skills from your course to a series of tasks. You will also need to undertake your own research to obtain the information required. The grading criteria covered by this assignment are shown in the box below.

Grading criteria

	Grading criteria	Evidence
P1	Describe the ethical issues a business needs to consider in its operational activities	Task 1
P2	Explain the implications for the business and stakeholders of a business operating ethically	Task 2
M1	Assess how a selected business could improve their operations ethically	Task 3
D1	Evaluate the impact of a selected business's ethical behaviour on stakeholders and the business	Task 4

YOUR ASSIGNMENT TASKS

Scenario

You are working as an executive's assistant at a firm of management consultants. Your manager, Andrea Tate, is keen that all the senior consultants who visit clients to discuss potential projects stress the business benefits of operating ethically. Your firm can help them to identify and achieve these goals. Andrea wants to cover this issue at the next in-house sales conference, but rather than talk generally about 'ethics' she wants to illustrate her points by referring to a particular business organisation. She has asked you to obtain the information she requires.

Carry out the tasks below and provide the information in the formats requested. Include a bibliography of all reference sources used during this assignment.

Task 1 (Pass criterion P1)

To provide the information required, you will need to investigate a business of your choice and identify its activities from an ethical point of view.

a) Select a business and give the reasons why you chose this particular business.

b) Describe the mission statement and corporate aims and objectives (or values and goals).

c) Describe the ethical issues the business needs to consider.

d) Describe how the business is attempting to show its stakeholders that it is aware of the ethical concerns that apply to its operational activities.

Note: You are advised to check with your tutor (who will play the part of Andrea) that your selected business will meet the criteria before you start this task.

Task 2 (Pass criterion P2)

Running a business ethically can have implications for stakeholders as well as for the business itself. Use the same business that you selected for Task 1 or an alternative business if you prefer.

a) Prepare a table which identifies the different stakeholders who are affected by the operations of your selected business.

b) For each type of stakeholder in the table, explain the benefits and drawbacks of the way the business currently operates giving reasons and examples to support your opinions.

c) Include any conflicts of interest between different stakeholders and give reasons for these differences below your table.

d) Explain the implications for the business itself of operating ethically.

Task 3 (Merit criterion M1)

Businesses need to look into ways they may improve their operations ethically. To give further information to the senior consultants at the next in-house conference, Andrea would like you to develop the research carried out so far. She would like you to:

a) Assess how your selected business could improve its operational activities to be more ethical and to have a positive impact on its operations.

b) Prepare a presentation of your assessment for Andrea to use at the in-house conference.

Task 4 (Distinction criterion D1)

Assessments of business operations ethical or otherwise should always be evaluated to establish the impact on the business and its stakeholders before final decisions are taken. Therefore, to support your presentation in Task 3:

a) Prepare a detailed report for Andrea to evaluate the effect of each of the changes and suggestions you recommended in Task 3 on each type of stakeholder *and* on your selected business.

b) Each of the conclusions you reach should be supported by appropriate evidence from your research.

PASS LEVEL ANSWERS

Louise Cole – Assignment 38.1, Task 1 (P1)

The organisation I have chosen to investigate is The Guide Dogs for the Blind Association. I have chosen this business because I think it is very ethical as it carries out an excellent and valuable service to help blind and severely visually impaired people to become mobile again with the help of a trained guide dog. It does wonderful work with dogs which I know because my aunt was a volunteer puppy walker for a long time.

I have copied the vision of Guide Dogs and its mission from its website at http://www.guidedogs.org.uk/aboutus and this is shown here.

OUR VISION

The Guide Dogs for the Blind Association (GDBA) wants a world in which all people who are blind and partially-sighted enjoy the same rights, opportunities and responsibilities as everyone else.

OUR MISSION

Our mission is to provide guide dogs, mobility and other rehabilitation services that meet the needs of blind and partially-sighted people. In addition, we also

- campaigns for the rights of people who are blind and partially-sighted,
- educates the public about eye care
- invests millions of pounds in eye disease research.

(From The Guide Dogs for the Blind Association website)

The main ethical issue that GDBA is involved with is equality for people who are blind and partially-sighted. I think that other ethical issues that GDBA needs to consider are as follows:

1   Where to get the dogs from, how to train them and what to do with them if they fail their training or are ill.

2   How to encourage applications from people who need a dog and how to train them to look after it – plus what to do if they haven't enough money to look after it or don't like animals or neglect it in some way.

3   How to raise and spend money to do all this because Guide Dogs doesn't get any money from the government, only from appeals and other gifts. It also needs to have enough money in reserve so that it doesn't have problems if it runs short of money for any reason. It must also obey the law about what it does with its money.

4 The other things it does and how it does them, such as its Travel Charter (below), the research project it did on street design and the campaigns it gets involved with. These must be right for the charity and not something that is disreputable.

GDBA tells people about its aims and what it does on its website. It also has a quarterly magazine *Forward,* has packs for teachers doing Citizenship. It also has a book, *Guide to Guide Dogs* which is all about guide dogs and gives lots of information to anyone who wants to work for them or become a volunteer.

The GDBA website includes a lot of information that relates to ethics even though it doesn't have an ethical policy, or at least there isn't one on the website. For example, they say that they campaign for the rights of the blind and partially-sighted community, especially on mobility and access issues. They also want more ethnic minority blind people to have dogs in the future. They breed over 1,000 guide dog puppies every year and only charge a new owner 50p to ensure no-one cannot have one because they have no money. Dogs who are unsuitable after training are found alternative careers (such as with the police) or found homes and when dogs retire they are placed with voluntary adopters. So every dog is always looked after as well as possible all its life.

GDBA wants their dogs to be welcomed on all forms of transport, without being charged, and has written a Travel Charter which it wants travel companies to sign up to. It wants staff who work for the travel companies to welcome the person and their dog and be helpful, such as by saying the name of the next destination on a bus, coach or train. This is also communicating ethical policies to other businesses.

GDBA has many fundraising days and holds lots of events so that everyone knows what it does. All these activities help to raise money and also help to raise the profile of Guide Dogs. It also encourages businesses to support it by recycling ink cartridges or old mobile phones. It also collects stamps. It doesn't say whether it does any recycling itself in its offices. On its website it also says that supporting a Guide Dog campaign can be good for businesses who want to do this as part of their own Corporate Social Responsibility.

Its campaigns have included campaigning for equal rights and it launched a fireworks petition before The Fireworks Act was passed, because fireworks can cause lots of stress to animals. GDBA also wants the government to spend more money in rehabilitating people who lose their sight. In 2007 it got involved with the 1 Million 4 Disability campaign, launched by the European Disability Forum.

Task 2 (P2) Stakeholders in Guide Dogs

Stakeholder	Benefits	Drawbacks
Owners	There are no owners of GDBA because it is a charity. But the managers are responsible for the way the business is run	Managers may not have enough money to do everything they want
Employees	Can work with dogs and be promoted from working in the kennels to training dogs and/or working with visually handicapped people	May have to work at weekends or during the holidays as dogs need looking after all the time
Dogs	Looked after all their lives and well trained	May be given to someone who doesn't like animals. This is why every owner is regularly visited by a Dog Care and Welfare Advisor who can check everything is all right
Volunteers and puppy walkers	Can work with dogs to help to look after them and support the Association	Don't get paid for what they do. May be upset when they have to hand over a puppy they have brought up
Customers – these are the dog owners	Will be more mobile because of the dog and also have companionship	Have to pay nominal 50p a week for its upkeep
Suppliers	Will be supplying a national organisation which is well known	May have to give discounts because all charities are careful with their money
Competitors	GDBA doesn't really have any competitors	
Citizens - these include local people who live near the kennels as well as the general public	They may be able to get involved in events and support GDBA	They may not like living near kennels if the dogs are noisy and barking at night

I think that the main conflicts could be between managers who want to save money and staff who want to spend money on the best facilities for the dogs and may want to train them for longer than managers would like. It must also be hard for staff if they don't like a new dog owner and trust him or her to look after the dog properly. Even though an advisor can visit, it may not be obvious if the dog is just being neglected a bit or not given much love or affection. Another conflict could be between local people who complain about the noise if the dogs are barking at night, especially if the kennels are in a residential area.

It is important that GDBA is ethical because it needs a good reputation to be able to attract funds from its supporters. People wouldn't give it money or leave it money in their will if they thought it wasn't ethical.

ASSESSOR FEEDBACK FORM

Learner Name: Louise Cole

Assignment Ref 38.1 – Tasks 1 and 2 (P1 and P2)

Louise, I was very interested to read your work, especially after our discussion about the differences you would face if you chose an organisation in the voluntary sector rather than one in the private sector which has the main aim of making a profit.

You have made a good start to this task and included many relevant factors which illustrate how Guide Dogs for the Blind Association operates and works to raise and spend money ethically. However, there are one or two gaps that you need to fill in before you achieve pass standard.

The first links to the discussion we had. Charities, just like other businesses, have to make sure that they comply with several laws and regulations particularly in relation to their finances. The trustees are responsible for this aspect of their operations and are key stakeholders in the business. You may remember that I suggested that you should check if the website contained an annual report and/or auditor's report and read these carefully. If you do this, you will be able to write about its legal and regulatory compliance in more detail than just saying 'it must obey the law'! You will also be able to add the trustees to the stakeholder table, rather than saying that 'no-one owns Guide Dogs'.

I think it is useful to separate 'managers' from 'employees' because they will have slightly different interests as you have said. Again, if you read the annual report carefully you will be able to give some examples and reasons to support your claims about managers. In the employees section, you should also try to look at working conditions more carefully – are GDBA as good at looking after their employees as the dogs? Do they have policies in relation to diversity, for example? You also need to see if they have any policies relating to their suppliers. It would be useful if you could make some comment about the business practices of GDBA – do they pay their suppliers promptly, for example? Especially small suppliers who would struggle to wait for payment. There is also GDBA own stance on issues such as the environment and sustainability that would be relevant here. You may find it helpful to check down the list of ethical issues we covered in class (see your scheme document for details, too) and match each one against information you have obtained on Guide Dogs for the Blind Association.

However, do remember that this is one reason why websites on their own can often prove inadequate if you need to find out about an organisation's policies in depth. You told me when we discussed your choice of Guide Dogs that you know someone who works there. I would recommend that you see if you can talk to him or her – or see if that person could arrange for you to talk to one of the local managers. Failing that, you could email their head office or telephone them. Primary research would add to your account significantly and would also prove invaluable for moving on to achieving Merit and Distinction criteria later.

Do remember to use your new information to build upon the work you have already done, which is fundamentally sound. Hopefully you will find that Guide Dogs for the Blind Association are only too pleased to help you if you contact them. As you rightly point out in your answer they are keen to foster a positive reputation because they need public support.

Remember, too, that GDBA also has to cope with other charities (and telethons like Children in Need or Red Nose Day) which all want public support. Therefore it needs to come up with innovative (but ethical) ways of raising money. This is an important aspect that all charities need to consider, i.e. competition from other worthy organisations which want money and support from the public. You need to investigate this in more detail to include in your revised answer, because it is simply not correct – from this point to view – to say that GDBA has no competition!

Finally – one further word of advice. You have chosen GDBA because you believe in its aims and what it does. This is good but it also means that you are apt to think with your heart rather than with your head! To assess its ethics you need to stand back a little bit and think about GDBA rather more dispassionately. Obtain facts about the way it operates and then assess these. To achieve M1 and D1 grading criteria you will need to think about whether it could make improvements to what it does and how it communicates its ethical stance – and you will only be able to do this effectively if you can think rather more objectively than you are doing at the moment.

I look forward to reading your revised work.

Adam Bell - Assignment 38.1, Task 1 (P1)

Introduction

For this business ethics assignment I have chosen to investigate Ryanair, which is now Europe's largest low fares airline. The reason is because Ryanair is incredibly successful, yet is frequently the subject of critical customer feedback and bad media reports. It has even been called the 'unacceptable and irresponsible face of capitalism'. I wanted to investigate whether this is mainly because of the aggressive style of its management, in particular its CEO Michael O'Leary, or if it is because the company itself operates in an unethical manner. I thought this was very relevant too because the airline industry as a whole is now being criticised on environmental grounds – yet Ryanair is saying it will expand its operations to offer flights to the US for only £7. Again I wanted to find more about this whole issue.

Ryanair mission statement

The Ryanair mission statement is as follows:

'To provide our customers with safe, good value, point-to-point air services. To effect and to offer a consistent and reliable product and fares appealing to leisure and business markets on a range of European routes. To achieve this we will develop our people and establish lasting relationships with our suppliers.'

Ryanair's goals

Ryanair's objective, in its online strategy document is as follows. 'To establish itself as Europe's leading low-fares scheduled passenger airline through continued improvements and expanded offerings of its low-fares service. It aims to offer low fares that generate increased passenger traffic while maintaining a continuous focus on cost-containment and operating efficiencies.'

Ryanair's main goal has always been to cut its operating costs to a minimum so that it can sell tickets cheaply. It aims to get passengers from A to B as cheaply as possible and many of its goals are focused on this, such as operating from cheap regional airports. It also wants to expand. In 2006 it carried a record 42.5 million passengers. It wants to increase this to 70 million by 2012. It has now announced plans to sell flight tickets to the US for only £7 and would like to take-over Aer Lingus, the Irish airline (in 2007 it owned 25%). It is also buying 117 more new aircraft, to increase its fleet of 107 Boeing 737-800s to 269 by 2012. It wants to increase its revenue and profits. Despite increases in fuel charges its expected net profit for 2007 is £257 million which will be an increase of 29% on 2006. Its revenues also increased by 33% because of a growth in passenger numbers, an increase in its average fares and other charges, such as for checked-in luggage.

How Ryanair operates

Ryanair sells tickets direct on its website. It discourages passengers from checking in baggage by charging them. Passengers with overweight bags must pay a surcharge. This means more passengers bring hand luggage only and this means Ryanair can process passengers more quickly from fewer check-in desks and pay less in baggage handling charges. This also helps to reduce the turn-round time between journeys as it is very important to keep this as short as possible. Ryanair uses cheap regional airports and prefers passengers to use online check-in and go straight to the departure gate. It sells travel insurance, hotel rooms and car rentals as well as scratch cards during the flight. All these bring it additional revenue and so do onboard purchases. It also introduced in-flight gambling in 2007.

It gives nothing free on its flights – although it sometimes gives away free one way tickets as a promotion. It charges for anything bought onboard. It also tried to charge disabled passengers for the use of wheelchairs but was taken to a tribunal by the Disability Rights Commission who won the case.

The ethical aspects Ryanair must consider

Ryanair has a Code of Business Conduct and Ethics. This is for its staff and is available online. It covers the following issues:

- **The working environment** at Ryanair, including protection for staff against discrimination and harassment; privacy of personal information of staff; Internet usage by staff; substance abuse by staff.

- **The business activities** of Ryanair, including being honest and fair to customers, obtaining best value from suppliers but also being open and truthful; disclosing results of operations in good time, fairly, understandably and accurately to shareholders. Ryanair also confirms it aims 'to provide a reasonable return on investment to shareholders by pursuing sound growth and earnings objectives while exercising prudence in the use of assets and resources.' It will not seek competitive advantage through illegal or unethical business practices and no employee must accept gifts, hospitalities or other benefits that could influence them or be construed as a bribe.

- **Financial reporting** is the next area. All company books and records must be true and complete and there are rules relating to access to company assets and how transactions are recorded as well as administrative and accounting controls. Ryanair is a publicly owned company and the company is committed to full compliance with all requirements applicable to its public disclosures.

- **Company property** must not be used by staff for personal benefit and all employees must safeguard confidential information about the company.

- **Conflict of interest**. This covers issues such as the type of other work an employee can do whilst working for Ryanair, the type of investments they have and job applications by friends and relatives as well as insider-trading in shares and transactions that involve relatives.

- **Laws and regulations**. This covers compliance with employment laws and regulations that apply in all the countries in which Ryanair operates, health and safety laws and regulations and environmental laws and regulations.

- **Disciplinary action** (when necessary) and **Reporting procedures** if staff have a query or problem.

However, there are other ethical issues Ryanair must consider because of the business it is in.

- **Safety** is a very important area. It doesn't matter how cheap the tickets are, if there was an accident because of poor maintenance or because the pilots weren't concentrating this would affect future business dramatically. Ryanair boasts on its website that in 30 years of operations it has not had a single incident involving major injury to passengers or flight crew. It says this is because it has safety training procedures, has invested in safety related equipment and has an internal confidential reporting system for safety issues. It also hires qualified maintenance personnel and provides proper training for them and maintains its aircraft in accordance with European industry standards. Ryanair stresses that its low cost operating strategy does not extend to the areas of maintenance, training or quality control.

- **The environment**. Ryanair argues that aviation accounts for less than 1.6% of greenhouse gas emissions. It claims it is Europe's greenest airline because it invests in the latest aircraft and engine technologies which significantly reduce fuel burn and CO_2 emissions. Because it has modern planes and operates from remote airports fewer people on the ground are affected by noise and there is less rubbish on each plane because there are no 'free' goods offered. (This also reduces the cleaning needed!) Ryanair is against making air travellers pay an environmental tax because it claims road transport is worse. It also said the government's increase in UK departure tax from £5 to £10 was just another tax on tourists.

- **Customer service**. Customers want to be treated politely and considerately especially if they have a problem, such as wanting to change a ticket or if a flight is delayed or cancelled. Air travellers may also have a claim about missing or damaged baggage. They may also be concerned about disabled access onto a plane and facilities on board (including cleanliness). They want flights to be punctual and Ryanair claims it is good in this respect and at the top of the European league. It also has fewer lost bags and cancellations than many other airlines.

- **Human rights** which includes the recruitment of staff and issues such as diversity and the right to join a trade union.

- **Corporate governance** This means that Ryanair must be run properly and use resources carefully and shareholders must be treated fairly. For example,

111

they must be able to stop directors trying to pay themselves too much money and they must also be able to see the accounts and other statements themselves each year (see Financial reporting above). Ryanair has stated it complies with the Combined Code which applies to companies listed on the Irish stock exchange as well as the London stock exchange. But in 2003 one investment fund said the company had failed to meet best practice as only one non-executive was independent and less than 20 days notice was given of the AGM which meant that shareholders didn't have enough time to read the report. As well, non-executive directors had been granted share options which aren't considered a suitable form a payment for their services. As well, its disclosure on environmental issues was not detailed enough. When I checked there was a full environmental statement where Ryanair claimed it was the greenest airline dated September 2006 so perhaps the situation has improved since then. I could find no other criticisms about its corporate governance online.

Ryanair communicates all information about its ethics from its website. It says it doesn't produce information packs to anyone because these cost money. Therefore the only way to find out information about the firm is online, but their website is comprehensive and has all the information stakeholders could need, including financial reports. Michael O'Leary is very defensive of the business's strategy in relation to aspects such as the environment and safety and the airline gets a lot of coverage in the national press. It has also been the subject of television programmes, some of which have been very critical.

Conflicts frequently occur at Ryanair between different groups of stakeholders. The senior management, mainly Mr O'Leary, is always fighting other groups, e.g. the Government and its tax, customers who want better service, staff who want more pay. He argues staff can leave and work elsewhere if they don't like it and that customers know what they are getting. This does not give them the right, though, to ignore people's basic rights, such as those of the disabled. The strength of opposition to Ryanair is shown in alternative websites, such as http://www.ryanaircampaign.org/ which includes dozens of negative press reports covering many different types of stakeholders.

This obviously concerns Ryanair because it has tried to get the site closed down and challenged the domain name. Ryanair knows it must be seen to be ethical, especially in key areas. This is why, when there were reports about rushed descents by pilots (rather than going around again which is safer) they quickly issued a statement which said that they disapproved of that practice and safety must be paramount. However, Ryanair also argues that they are in the business of providing the cheapest fares and that they must keep costs low to do this. In the investor's part of the website they stress their commitment to highly qualified pilots who are paid more than the average wage, new aircraft and safety as well as other ethical policies. This is because they know that investment, as well as passenger numbers, is crucial for their future expansion plans.

Task 2 (P2)

Type of Stakeholder	Benefit	Reason/example	Drawbacks	Reason/example
Investor/owner	Make money out of their investment	Shares have generally increased in value and in 2007 experts were saying they are a good buy	No dividends paid on ordinary shares	This is because Ryanair retains future earnings to pay for additional aircraft and for its expansion programme
Passenger	Save money on flights	Can fly very cheaply all around Europe, sometimes for nothing	Remote airports, no 'frills', hard to get money back if there is a problem	Many websites contain blogs and complaints about Ryanair customer service
Employee	Protection against	See ethical policy for staff. Ryanair claims its pilots are the best paid in Europe and have no overnight stays away	High productivity targets to achieve. Cabin crew have to pay for their own training and it is deducted from their first year's salary	Some pilots and cabin crew have complained about fast turn-round times
Supplier	Policy of treating suppliers fairly	See ethical policy	Costs – anything supplied will have to be good value	Ryanair keeps its costs as low as possible
Competitor	It can lose customers to its competitors	Ryanair often gets bad publicity which puts people off	It can be difficult to beat in some areas	Its safety and punctuality records are both very good and it is cheaper than most competitors
Citizens	According to Ryanair, it is more 'friendly' to citizens than other airlines	This is because it uses remote airports so there is less noise and also because it has newer planes and doesn't make as much rubbish.	Environmentalists don't like Ryanair, nor do unions. The Government and EU are probably wary too because of Ryanair's campaigns about tax and other issues.	Cheap flights mean more travellers and Ryanair plans to expand. Ryanair is anti-union – see www.ryan-be-fair.org set up by the International Transport Workers Federation

ASSESSOR FEEDBACK FORM

Learner Name: Adam Bell
Assignment Ref 38.1 – Tasks 1 and 2 (P1 and P2)

Adam, you have obviously taken a lot of time and trouble over your research for this assignment, for which you must be congratulated. You have looked beyond the headlines, which is important, to identify some of the key issues that are relevant to business ethics at Ryanair.

I was interested in your reason for choosing Ryanair and I am pleased that you have managed to keep a balance between the negative publicity the business often receives and other positive facts about the company.

Your information was set out clearly under appropriate headings, which meant it was easy to read. You have identified and accurately described a wide range of ethical issues that apply to your chosen business and have certainly met the criteria for P1.

In Task 2, you have applied your findings to different stakeholders. I was slightly disappointed that you had kept to the example stakeholder list in the scheme, which meant that you have some unexpected groupings, such as 'government' under 'citizens'. You would have done better to expand this list – for example, managers could have been dealt with separately to other employees – or perhaps Mr O'Leary, with his combative business style, could have been an item on his own!

Despite that, I was pleased to see that you have included a wide range of examples to support your claims. You have also identified some relevant conflicts of interest although these could have been broadened rather more. Again, this might have been easier if you had identified a broader range of stakeholders.

You have appropriately identified the importance to Ryanair of being seen to be an ethical business on crucial aspects of its operations, such as safety, the environment and how it treats its staff and customers.

I look forward to seeing how you assess the improvements Ryanair could make to achieve M1 grading criterion and certainly there is a considerable amount of material you can usefully evaluate to achieve D1 grading criterion.

MERIT LEVEL ANSWERS

Aysha Bhamra – Assignment 38.1, Task 3 (M1)

Slide one

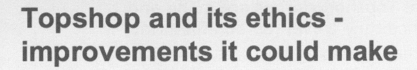

Topshop and its ethics - improvements it could make

Aysha Bhamra

1

Slide two

Topshop today

○ Topshop is very successful
○ It sells fashion clothes
○ It could be more ethical in the way it operates

2

Slide three

Ethical issues

o Where Topshop clothes are made and distance they travel (carbon footprint)
o The cheap clothing business (use and throw away)
o Trading fairly and suppliers/workers (not paid living wage etc)
o Equality (eg size of clothes stocked)
o Business practices
o Tax

3

Slide four

Its competitors

o These include
  • Next
  • River Island
  • Primark
  • Matalan
  • New Look
  • French Connection
  • H&M
  • Zara

According to Labour behind the Label and Clean up Fashion - Next, Zara, New Look and H&M are all more ethical than Topshop.

4

Slide five

What it could do

Stock clothes over size 16 because at the moment they discriminate against heavier people.

The Kate Moss collection makes this worse as only thin people can wear her type of clothes. Some young girls will have to diet a lot to wear them. Also her lifestyle is not a good example to young girls.

5

Slide six

What it could do also

o Join the Ethical Trading Initiative (This applies to all Arcadia businesses, not just Topshop) and make sure suppliers/workers are treated properly.

o Stock more fair trade clothes (they only stock a few by People Tree at the moment)

6

Slide seven

It should also

o Not encourage young people to buy and throw away clothes

o Look at more recycling

o Look at what clothes are made of, eg are they organic cotton

o Not move clothes all around the world because of the carbon footprint

o Have an ethical audit

7

Slide eight

What the owner could do

o He is Sir Philip Green and is worth billions.

o He saved £285 million in tax, according to the *Money Programme*, because he lives in Monaco part of the year

o He has big parties. He spent about £20 million and took over a Maldive island for his friends for his 55th birthday, flying them all there. This is not good for the environment.

o He should move to England and pay tax here, where his customers are.

8

Slide nine

Conclusion 1

o Taking action would mean pressure groups like Clean up Fashion and Labour Behind the Label would give Arcadia a better ethical score

o Clothes would be available for a wider range of customers and that could increase sales

o The press would stop criticising Philip Green for living abroad and his taxes would help the British economy.

9

Slide ten

Conclusion 2

o One report said Topshop is working on writing its Corporate social responsibility report but this is no good unless it takes action.

o It could stock more clothes made from organic cotton that are made nearer here to reduce its carbon footprint.

10

ASSESSOR FEEDBACK FORM

Learner Name: Aysha Bhamra

Assignment ref 38.1, Task 3 (M1)

You have obviously worked hard on your presentation Aysha and I particularly liked the way you had enlivened some of the slides with appropriate illustrations.

When you did Tasks 1 and 2 to achieve P1 and P2, you identified some of the main ethical issues that fashion retailers need to look at and those that concern pressure groups such as Labour Behind the Label – such as where fashion retailers source their clothes and how the workers who make them are treated and paid. These are important issues which are part of the Ethical Trading Initiative – which you unfortunately failed to identify properly in your presentation. You really should have explained what the ETI is and how joining it should mean Topshop is more rigorous in its ethical stance to the labour it uses. This is the main benefit of joining – not because Topshop will not get criticised as much!

Unfortunately the ETI and labour force/supply chain issues were rather lost in the middle of your presentation because you introduced other concerns – such as clothes sizes, how far they travel and points relating to Philip Green.

It would have been better to identify actions that other retailers have taken (e.g. Next, New Look and H&M) which Topshop has not. Remember, too, that Topshop is part of the Arcadia group and you do not make it clear in your presentation whether you are concerned with the ethics of just Topshop or the whole group. For example, any tax to be paid by Sir Philip Green would be on the profits of the Arcadia Group, not just Topshop – although really Philip Green's private life is not very relevant to the ethical business issues you are addressing, no matter what your personal feelings are! Also, when you are comparing Topshop with its direct competitors, this should probably not include Primark and Matalan which sell clothes more cheaply than Topshop.

I suggest that you change your presentation a little by identifying the main operational issues that you think Topshop should improve – not Philip Green himself! Then explain and assess each one, starting with those you think are the most important for the business. Also, do remember to be specific! For example, if you say Topshop is 'very successful' then state its last profit figure and how many shops there are.

Remember, too, that you do not need to go into great detail on a slide because you should not be reading from it! Instead, just put the key information that will remind you what to say. At the end, try to have one conclusion slide which summarises your key points. I am sure that with a little work to organise your ideas more logically you should have no problems in soon achieving M1.

Adam Bell – Assignment 38.1, Task 3 (M1)

Slide one

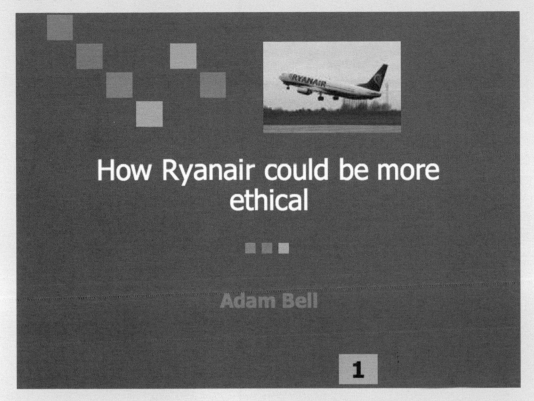

How Ryanair could be more ethical

Adam Bell

1

Slide two

Aim of this presentation

- To assess the scope for ethical improvements at Ryanair, based on its current operational practices.
- To suggest changes Ryanair could make that would contribute to ethical behaviour and have a positive impact on its operations.

2

Slide three

Recommended changes and improvements

- Publicise an up-to-date environmental policy
- Review extra charges and give better customer care and service
- Improve conditions for staff
- Stop having misleading adverts
- Have ethical policies for dealing with disabled passengers
- Meet best practice for corporate governance
- Prepare a CSR report

3

Slide four

Publicise an up-to-date environmental policy

- The airline already claims it is 'green' because it replaces planes every 2.5 years so uses new technology but many people might not know this
- The UK government has to reduce CO_2 emissions and needs the help of all industry
- Competitors have adopted this idea (eg Virgin) whereas Ryanair has just argued that the contribution of airlines to global warming is negligible
- Publicising a positive, up-to-date policy would be good PR and cost very little

4

Slide five

Review charges and give better customer care and service

- Reduce excess charges for extras including 'jumping' the queue, checking in baggage and everything bought on board. Most no frills operators to Europe do this but Ryanair charges more than most.
- Reduce prices of associated services eg hotels, car hire to give customers a better deal.
- Scrap premium phone line for customer contact and/or allow contact by email.
- Reduce/scrap £14 admin fee for handling complaints.
- Train staff better and discipline any who are rude to customers.

5

Slide six

Improve conditions for staff

- Recognise Irish Airline Pilots Association (trade union).
- Stop being penny pinching and let staff recharge their mobile phones at work
- Pay for training of flight attendants. At present Ryanair pays it in advance but then claims it back each month out of their first year's salary
- Don't put staff under such pressure to meet targets that they have to leave or resort to complaining online.

6

Slide seven

Stop having misleading adverts

- Employ professional agency to create adverts
- Don't advertise free or £0 tickets which leave off the tax so people don't realise there are extra costs

7

Slide eight

Have ethical policy for dealing with disabled passengers

- Don't charge for wheelchair use. This is important because of the Disability Discrimination Act
- Train staff to deal properly with sick or ill passengers.

8

Slide nine

Meet best practice for corporate governance

- Comply with the Combined Code
- Do more than the minimum – aim to equal best practice. This is important now that Ryanair is an established, profitable business.

9

Slide ten

Prepare a CSR report

- Corporate Social Responsibility shows that a business is trying to do more than the basics about ethical issues.
- Ryanair does not have a CSR report and preparing one would highlight important ethical issues and help to show it takes its responsibilities seriously.

10

Slide eleven

Summary

- If Ryanair made some of the recommended changes it would operate more ethically.
- Operating ethically can often be very beneficial for a business, especially a well-established, highly profitable business like Ryanair

11

ASSESSOR FEEDBACK FORM

Learner Name: Adam Bell
Assignment ref 38.1, Task 3 (M1)

I found your presentation very interesting Adam, as it built upon the work you did for P1 and P2.

I liked your Introduction because this clearly said what you were aiming to achieve in your presentation. You then focused on specific areas where you feel there is scope for improvement with some general reasons to support your arguments. This is always far more effective than trying to include too much.

I was pleased that you mentioned that most, no frills, operators, like Ryanair, charge for baggage now. This type of information will be important when you are evaluating your ideas for the Distinction criterion D1.

Your summary, too, was succinct and to the point.

I was a little disappointed that you only used one illustration at the start of the presentation, as this would have broken up the text more. Also, it is worth remembering that you don't need to go into too much detail on a slide, because you can add the details for the audience when you talk. The slide should really be just a summary of the main points.

That said, you spoke clearly and at the right pace and made eye contact with the audience when you were talking. You had obviously thought about questions that you might be asked in advance and answered these confidently. You also managed to smile, which was good!

I was a little concerned that when you were asked about your research you seem to have relied heavily on the Wikipedia website. This is always risky unless you check the original sources, as I am sure you are aware, because anyone can contribute to Wikipedia! For example, you can cross-check any issues relating to misleading advertisements to the ASA website.

You have certainly achieved M1 with this presentation and I will be interested to read your report to achieve the Distinction criterion D1, when you must evaluate these suggested changes. Remember, too, that you will also need to include a list of your reference sources – as a bibliography – which should go beyond Wikipedia or the Ryanair website!

Marek Janicki – Assignment 38.1, Task 4 (D1)

REPORT ON ETHICAL IMPROVEMENTS THAT BARCLAYS BANK COULD MAKE

Introduction

The Fraser Ethical Reputation Index ranks companies with high public profiles according to the public's perception of their ethics. The higher the rating the least ethical the company. According to a report in the *Independent* newspaper in 2006, Barclays is number five in that list.

This means people think it isn't ethical. Only McDonald's, Nike, Shell and Adidas came out worse, which is one reason I have picked Barclays out of all the other high street banks, although many ethical issues that relate to Barclays also relate to them, too.

Despite this, in May 2007 Barclays was given a Platinum rank and came second in the Business in the Community index published in the Sunday Times. This index is based on a self-assessment survey which has to be signed by the company's chief executive. Barclays chief executive is John Varley who says he wants the business to be leaders in corporate responsibility. But the business was highlighted in a *Whistleblower* programme by the BBC and the staff weren't acting ethically then. That is another reason why I picked Barclays.

In this report I list the issues that Barclays should tackle and say how these would affect different stakeholders and the business.

Ethical issues

Ethical issues that businesses like Barclays need to consider are as follows:

- **Corporate governance**, so that shareholders and investors are treated fairly and the company is run properly.

- **Corporate social responsibility**, which means doing more than the minimum in different ethical areas relating to stakeholders, such as looking after employees and customers and being honest and open with suppliers and shareholders.

- **Environment**, which includes things like climate change and global warming and looks at things like being carbon neutral.

- **Sustainability**, which means operating without using up scarce resources that will make things difficult for the next generation. An example is using renewable energy, such as electricity from wind farms.

- **Human rights**, which means respecting the rights of all other people no matter who they are.

- **Corruption**, which means everyone being honest in every way.

- **Trading fairly**, which means not misleading customers or suppliers.

- **Legal and ethical compliance**, which means obeying all the laws and regulations that apply to that type of business and its operations.

- **Business practices**, which refers to how the business operates from recording its transactions to training its staff.

- **Working conditions**, which refers to the conditions in which the staff work and what they are expected to do, how long they work each week, the hours they work and how much they are paid.

- **Individual ethical responsibilities**, which means how individual staff at all levels treat the people they deal with. For example, if they have a difficult problem will they try to help or not? And will they sell a product that will earn them more commission even if this would not help the customer? This includes people working in call centres as well as people working for the business itself.

Banks and ethical issues

Banks are often accused of acting unethically. In March 2007 the Office of Fair Trading announced it was studying retail bank pricing because people cannot work out what it costs them to have a personal current account. Many people think these are free but really this is not the case. Plus banks use current accounts to try to sell other products. The OFT has received many complaints about unauthorised overdraft charges and other fees which are more expensive than necessary and is investigating this. In addition it thinks the banks are not competitive, which is important, because if they were the prices of different products would be more obvious and more competitive. On the BBC website it says that the true cost of bouncing a cheque may be less than £2 but banks charge people £25.

This is not the first time there have been problems with banks. Many banks are repaying large sums that they have charged customers who are overdrawn and/or cannot pay a direct debit. These are far more than are necessary than the amount necessary to cover the cost of sorting out the problem. Banks are trying to settle this dispute before it goes to court because then there would be a judgement they would all have to follow. One man got back £35,988 from Natwest which said it only settled the case to save large legal costs! To help people, the Consumer Action Group website has standard letters people can download to claim their money back. Or people can use the government's Money Claim Online service.

Banks are always trying to get money without their customers knowing. They charge for people withdrawing money from cash machines abroad and for buying things abroad. But they don't make it clear what those charges are. Robert Peston's report on the BBC website said using a debit card abroad from NatWest could cost a family from £20 to £120 for one trip in bank charges. And sending money abroad is expensive. My friend did that and it cost £20 just for his bank to complete a form. They also keep money in the banking system for days when it is being transferred. My uncle, who lives in Canada, says they don't have that problem because the money has to be transferred immediately whereas in the UK banks keep hold of it to make money on it.

It makes it worst, too, that banks make record profits. Barclays is up by 35% and a lot of that will be by charging people penalty charges or getting them to borrow money they don't need or can't afford. Banks are often trying to tempt people to take out credit cards and spend money or doing balance transfers, which just encourages people to stay in debt, or to take out huge mortgages and loans. This is unethical. Citizens Advice has said that they now see twice as many people to help them with debt as they did eight years ago. The BBC website says the average amount people owe is £13,153 but most are on very low incomes and don't understand the financial decisions they make. My cousin, who works in Germany, says they are not allowed to do that in Germany so they shouldn't be able to do it here.

Often this is deliberate mis-selling as was shown in the *Whistleblower* programme shown by the BBC in 2007 when BBC reporters worked undercover for Barclays for 9 months and found customers being misled, lied to and charged for financial products they didn't know they had. It was the same at the call centre and in the branch. All employees were focused on making targets to earn a bonus, often by changing the customer's current account from a free one to a chargeable one and hoping they wouldn't notice. I think this type of thing probably goes on all the time by all the banks.

Improvements Barclays could make

Banks have a lot of money, so they can afford to produce lots of literature which says how ethical they are whether they are or not. Barclays has a 64 page CSR report and it has lots of policies and principles, e.g. on animal experimentation, bribery and corruption, defence sector, equality and diversity charter, environmental policy statement, environmental and social impact assessment and human rights. It also could use this information to get a high score in the self-assessment survey in the Business in the Community index.

Despite all this I still think people won't trust it after the *Whistleblower* programme. Also many people don't like dealing with call centres and this again was shown in the TV programme because call centre staff are just in it for the money and don't care about the people they speak to. In the programme they enjoyed misleading them.

Barclays may not be any worse than other banks but I think it puts profits ahead of its customers. Its profits for 2006 were 35% higher than the year before and were a record £7.14bn. And it made this money even though it had to write-off more than £2 billion from Barclaycard customers. It now says it is more careful about the customers it takes on and refuses 60% of applications.

Like free banking and illegal charges the banks have also been criticised by the OFT for making late payment charges and these are now illegal.

Evaluation of action Barclays should take and effect on stakeholders

- Get rid of its call centres and employ more staff in branches to help customers. This would be good for the staff who are stakeholders and also for the customers who are stakeholders.

- Get rid of targets for staff based on selling financial products and get rid of bonuses for selling, too. This, again, would benefit both the staff and the customers, both of whom are stakeholders.

- Never persuade people to have a credit card or an overdraft or mortgage that they cannot afford. This would be good for customers and also for organisations like Citizens Advice which would have less work to do because not as many people would have problems.

- Explain exactly what all the charges are with all current accounts and make these as low as possible. This would benefit customers but may reduce the profits which the shareholders might not like but Barclays makes enough profit so that they would not be too badly affected.

- Stop charging for transactions made overseas. Nationwide doesn't do this so Barclays could afford not to. Again customers would benefit when they go abroad.

- Transfer money more quickly. Customers would benefit, both private customers and businesses.

Conclusion

I think all banks should do this but Barclays could set a lead, especially as it says it wants to be a leader when it comes to ethics. It has enough profits so that it wouldn't matter if it made a few million less. In fact, if it took the lead on ethical banking it could get twice as many customers who would leave the other banks and the shareholders would like this.

Marek Janicki   10 May 2007

ASSESSOR FEEDBACK FORM

Learner Name: Marek Janicki
Assignment ref 38.1, Task 4 (D1)

Marek, I read your report with interest, especially after the good work you did for P1 and P2, when you looked at the ethical issues Barclays needs to consider and then explained the implications for banks and their stakeholders. Also, in your presentation for M1, you focused on the key issues that you had researched relating to Barclays Bank.

Your Introduction was good with useful information on the Fraser Ethical Reputation Index. You also picked up the apparently contradictory findings of Barclays ranking in the Business in the Community index and the *Whistleblower* report. It was a little disappointing that you didn't investigate this in more detail in relation to Barclays stakeholders as this would have been very interesting.

Unfortunately you then listed all the different ethical issues that might apply to any business which wasn't required here. Instead you should have focused on the operations of your chosen organisation that you identified in your presentation as appropriate for ethical improvement.

One way to do this would have been to construct the main part of the report under appropriate ethical headings, then go into more detail about each one and its effect on stakeholders (both positive and negative) and then select those areas which you think are the most important and relevant to the bank.

Your next section focused on describing in detail many current ethical issues relating to banking. Much of this related to several banks, not just Barclays. Only the *Whistleblower* programme related just to Barclays – but it is dangerous to use just one source as a key focus for a conclusion without any other collaborative evidence. You did highlight some very relevant points but you needed to identify those which directly relate to Barclays operations. Instead your two examples both related to NatWest!

Another point to note, Marek, is that you need to make sure you research and provide facts, rather than opinions or allegations (such as your uncle's or sister's opinions, for example). You should also avoid sweeping generalisations which are unsubstantiated, such as 'All employees are . . . ' or 'I think this goes on all the time' which lessens the impact of the facts you have discovered. I would also recommend using a wide range of sources when you research. Apart from one or two other sources such as the *Independent* and the *Sunday Times* you appear to have used the BBC website almost exclusively for this report. Good research means checking out several different sources and comparing them and I would certainly have expected more reference to the Barclays website. You also need to list your reference sources clearly at the end of your report.

You do have some good ideas, however, for how Barclays could be seen by its customers to be a more ethical bank. However, you have not evaluated the scope for your suggested improvements, which is what was needed! This means thinking about the feasibility of each idea in relation to Barclays operations and its aims and objectives. For example, it is well known that customers are often apathetic about changing their bank. This may be one reason why the banks feel there is no percentage in changing their behaviour. You may also find it useful to compare the allegations made in the *Whistleblower* programme with the statements in Barclay's ethical policies, which you investigated in Task 1, and to analyse the factors which enabled Barclays to be ranked so highly in the Business in the Community index. You briefly mentioned that Barclays CEO was committed to ethical leadership but failed to investigate or refer to this at all when you reached the stakeholder section!

To achieve D1 you need to evaluate the effect of your suggestions on *each type* of stakeholder. Start by identifying all the stakeholder groups and then identify benefits to support your ideas as well as disadvantages to different groups. To do this you need to look at Barclays operations in more detail. For example, do its profits come mainly from high street banking or from wholesale banking? How does it spend its money (e.g. in tax, employing people, providing online services etc)? What are the benefits of its current operations to customers who can manage their money properly? For example, one argument could be that there should be greater protection for people who cannot manage their own money, rather than everyone in society – and that this is the job of the government, not individual banks. You may not agree with this, but thinking about things differently is all part of the evaluation process.

You will need to rework your ideas, looking specifically at Barclays and evaluating these to achieve D1. One way to start would be to write a brief evaluation of one or two of your ideas and check with me that you are doing this correctly before you carry on. If you do this, I am confident that you will be able to make the necessary changes to your report to achieve D1.

Adam Bell - Assignment 38.1 Task 4 (D1)

REPORT ON HOW RYANAIR COULD IMPROVE ITS OPERATIONS ETHICALLY

Introduction

This report evaluates the effect of the improvements that Ryanair could make to improve its operations ethically. It does this by identifying the effect upon specific groups of stakeholders as well as on the business itself. All the claims that are made are supported by researched evidence, and a list of sources is attached to this report.

Stakeholders and Ryanair

Stakeholders in Ryanair include the shareholders, the managers, employees, passengers, suppliers, competitors, citizens, the government and environmental pressure groups.

Each of them will be affected in different ways if Ryanair makes changes to the way in which it operates.

Areas identified for improvement

Scope for improvement has been identified in each of the following areas.

- **Publicise an up-to-date environmental policy**

  Although Ryanair claims it is Europe's greenest airline[1], it has not responded positively to new concerns that the aviation industry should help to reduce pollution. The Department of Transport forecasts that passenger numbers will more than double by 2030[2], which means that its CO_2 emissions will double also. It is no use business and industry and private people doing their best if all the gains are wiped out by the airlines.

  Several things could happen as a result. Passengers may start to be more aware of their 'carbon footprint' and limit their overseas travel or travel more by train or car. Also, Ryanair, and other airlines, are likely to find themselves in the spotlight more by pressure groups such as Greenpeace and Friends of the Earth because of the amount of fuel they use and the fact that their passengers are usually taking 'unnecessary' journeys. This may make people feel guilty so that they buy fewer flight tickets.

  If they don't, the government could tax air travel more to stop people flying as often – and this will probably affect budget travellers more than business travellers or the very rich, who can afford to pay tax more easily. On a cheap Ryanair flight the tax can be far more than the ticket. This is why Michael O'Leary denounced the doubling of UK departure tax as 'regressive, unfair and penal' and criticised the chancellor, Gordon Brown[3]. Or passengers could choose to fly with the more environmentally friendly airlines.

Michael O'Leary argued that airlines aren't the biggest contributor to global warming[4] but he is out of step with the way people think. Virgin Atlantic announced it would try to save up to two tonnes of fuel per flight by towing aircraft to runways so that engines don't run for as long. And Richard Branson pledged £1.6 bn of Virgin Group profits towards renewable energy initiatives. He also said that up to 25% of the world's aviation carbon dioxide emissions could be cut if airlines, airports and governments worked together[5]. This is a more positive response than Michael O'Leary who denied airplanes responsibility because he said aviation accounts for just 2% of CO^2 emissions and took out a huge advert in the Guardian to say how greedy Gordon Brown was[6].

In its environmental statement online Ryanair says it replaces its planes every 2.5 years and claims it is excellent at other environmental aspects, such as reducing fuel burn and CO^2 emissions but people don't know this, instead they read the headlines Mr O'Leary makes, whereas Richard Branson is more positive and tells people he is taking these concerns seriously and doing something about it. Ryanair should do the same and make it quite clear it will take an ethical stance on the environment in the future.

Effect on stakeholders of improvements in this area

Passengers: may be more loyal to Ryanair and won't feel as guilty if they make a trip.
Shareholders: could claim they invest in ethical funds.
Managers: cost of environmental policy should not affect profits yet will give good publicity.
Competitors: like Virgin Atlantic, would not get the better of Ryanair so easily.
Pressure groups: will not pursue Ryanair as much.
Government: may not tax travel more which would be more damaging to future ticket sales.

- **Review extra charges and give better customer care and service**

All airlines depend upon passengers for their business. They need to be customer focused and treat people fairly and honestly, otherwise they will lose business to their competitors.

Ryanair needs more passengers if it is to meet its expansion targets and be Europe's leading, low fares airline[7]. It also has a Code of Business Conduct and Ethics and a Passenger Charter[8] but it is still often arrogant and high-handed in the way it treats them. This might have been all right in its early days but now Ryanair has more competitors things are different. There are pages and pages of problems online at comparison travel sites like Ciao[9] and airlinequality.com[10] that people have had, far more than for competitors such as easyJet or Zoom.

Ryanair was one of the first to pass all its costs on to its customers to make a profit. In 2007 it made record profits and these increased by 30% in one quarter and a main reason was because it had introduced charges for passengers who wanted to check in baggage[11]. So it now appears more greedy when it keeps finding more and more ways of getting money out of passengers. According to a report in *Which* magazine[12], most no-frills European airlines charge passengers to check-in baggage and for excess baggage, but Ryanair charges more than anyone else because easyJet allows one free hold bag and flybe charges less and so does bmibaby. Virgin Atlantic doesn't charge at all and Richard Branson has announced his intention to fly passengers across the Atlantic as cheap as Ryanair. If Ryanair charges for bags they will not be competitive and the *Which* report said that most passengers would opt for an airline that doesn't charge for luggage if they had a choice.

Passengers also have to pay if they want to queue jump to get a good seat with their partner and for anything they buy onboard as well as extra if they pay for travel insurance by credit or debit card – but they also have to do this with easyJet. But when all this is added to the government taxes and other airport charges it can become expensive to fly with Ryanair, even if the ticket itself is cheap or sold as 'free'. A business reviewer in the *Times* said that this could eventually damage the Ryanair brand.[13]

A *Times* investigation also found that both Ryanair and easyJet have a huge mark up on their Scratchcards and give only 1% to good causes; they also make large profits by advertising cheap car hire and other services but sell these at inflated prices. This is not good publicity for either business[14].

If, on top of that, the staff are rude or if people are left to find their own way home if a flight is cancelled or if they cannot make a claim in time if their luggage is lost because they are on holiday then they will change their airline. There are many reports online at airlinequality.com and skyscrapercity.com and Ryanair is the only airline to have a campaign against it online which its lawyers have tried to close down at www.ryanaircampaign.org.

Because of EU regulations Ryanair now has to provide accommodation or meal vouchers if flights are delayed or cancelled but it has introduced an administration fee of £14 per ticket for handling refunds and, according to Wikipedia, Norwegian consumer authorities have fined Ryanair £43,000 for doing this[15]. Customers can only contact Ryanair by premium phone line, too and complain they are kept waiting for ages to make a simple mistake or have to keep ringing back. The more profits Ryanair makes the less customers will tolerate this sort of thing.

Competitors are increasing – approximately 60 new low-cost airlines were formed in 2004 according to Wikipedia and more have appeared since then. The more choice passengers have the more they will choose to go with an airline that treats them well in addition to being cheap.

Even if Ryanair sticks to all its extra charges to pay for its cheap tickets there is no need to make life difficult for people to contact them or to make a valid complaint. Also, there is no excuse for staff to behave badly or be rude and this does not save the airline money at all!

Effect on stakeholders of improvements in this area

Passengers will get a better quality service and experience and be more tempted to use Ryanair again.
Managers may save money advertising if passengers are more loyal and there will be less damaging press coverage.
Shareholders may gain if passenger numbers increase, even if the costs of customer service rise a little bit.
Staff will find they have fewer complaints to deal with and fewer annoyed customers to cope with.
Competitors may find that they lose business to Ryanair.

- **Improve conditions for staff**

Ryanair refuses to tolerate the idea of trade unions and does not recognise the Irish Airline Pilots' Association. In July 2006 an Irish High Court judge found that Ryannair had bullied pilots to force them to agree to new contracts and some Ryanair managers had given false evidence in court[16]. According to the Ryan Be Fair website[17], working conditions aren't good, for example office staff cannot recharge their mobile phones at work and flight attendants have to pay for all their own training costs. Ryanair will pay for this upfront but then the worker has to pay them back out of their first year's wages.

Employees at Ryanair have to work very hard to meet targets[18] – such as the 25 minute turn-round times and if they are not treated well either then this is not ethical.

Michael O'Leary argues that if anyone doesn't like working at Ryanair they are free to leave – apparently one poster just says 'If you don't like the company then get out[19]', but that ignores the fact that good, motivated and committed staff are not easy to find and recruitment can be costly if staff turnover is high.

Effect on stakeholders of improvements in this area

Passengers are more likely to find that staff are well trained, courteous and eager to help them.

Staff will be more motivated and keen to work for the company.

Managers will gain if people are keener to work for them and turnover is less.

Shareholders will gain if recruitment costs fall and the reputation of the business improves because this will help profits.

Suppliers may gain if they regularly deal with staff.

Competitors will find it harder to poach staff and will find the competition tougher.

- **Stop having misleading advertising**

Ryanair produces all its own adverts and doesn't have an agency[20] and some Irish newspapers say Michael O'Leary writes most of them himself, particularly those that attack people he doesn't like. Ryanair has been in trouble for misleading advertisements relating to prices several times. For example it advertised seats at £0 or for free when customers still have to pay tax and airport charges. There are several examples on the Advertising Standards Authority website of Ryanair adverts where complaints about misleading information have been upheld[21].

Ryanair has argued that some complaints are from competitors and that rarely do passengers actually complain. All they want are cheap seats. When Michael O'Leary is now saying they will fly to USA for £7 he is ignoring all the extra costs, such as tax, which still misleads the public.

Effect on stakeholders of improvements in this area

Passengers and **citizens** will be able to trust the claims that Ryanair makes.

Shareholders and managers should benefit from increased business and less bad publicity.

Competitors will have fewer opportunities to criticise Ryanair or report it to the ASA.

- **Have an ethical policy for dealing with disabled passengers**

People are less tolerant of discrimination now and expect businesses to take account of the reasonable needs of their employees and customers. These include airlines even though it seems they don't come under the Disability Discrimination Act yet according to the Disability Rights Commission[22]. Newspaper headlines relating to issues such as disabled customers being charged for wheelchairs or limiting the number of disabled passengers on a flight seem petty and make a business seem out of step with modern thinking. This is especially true when a business is successful, like Ryanair.

In addition the business has received negative publicity for staff being offhand or rude to people who are ill or injured, as well as disabled[23].

The airline is still being unfair to disabled passengers and as a result an MP,

Sharon Hodgson, brought an early day motion in Parliament which said

> 'That this House is outraged that Ryanair does not allow disabled customers the opportunity to state their requirements when booking flights electronically but instead chooses to insist that disabled customers must contact the company directly on an 0871 telephone number which costs 10 pence per minute; believes that this shows a lamentable attitude towards accommodating disabled passengers; and urges Ryanair to incorporate disabled customers into their normal online service forthwith'[24].

With Ryanair profits high this type of behaviour just gives the business a very bad name.

Effect on stakeholders of improvements in this area

Passengers would know that if they were disabled they would have no problems and would be treated fairly.
Staff would find it easier as they would be trained what to do to work ethically.
Shareholders and managers would gain because the reputation of the business would be better and more disabled people would buy tickets.
Suppliers could benefit, such as people who run hotels which specialise in disabled access as they could link to Ryanair and sell hotel rooms.

- **Meet best practice for corporate governance**

This is important because Ryanair depends upon shareholder loyalty and needs investors being attracted by share gains so that they continue to invest in the business. Ryanair says it has complied with the Combined Code since 2004[25] but a report online by West Midlands Pensions said it failed to meet best practice in 2003[26]. If many shareholders lost confidence in the business and sold their shares simultaneously the price would fall and Ryanair would not be able to meet its expansion targets without borrowing large sums of money. Also Mr O'Leary is at present trying to convince shareholders that buying Aer Lingus would be a good thing[27]. Shareholders will not support him if there is any suspicion that the company was not being run properly or if they thought they were being misled. They may be suspicious, for example, that no-one can stand up to Mr O'Leary. If they really approve of his management style then they may be worried that Ryanair is a one-man business and there is no-one who can follow him.

Whatever their beliefs, Ryanair should meet best practice of the Combined Code at all times now it is a well-established profitable company.

Effect on stakeholders of improvements in this area

Shareholders would have confidence in the business and that the money was being used efficiently and in accordance with the law.

The government (both Irish and UK) would know that Ryanair was a reputable business.

Managers and staff would know that their jobs were safe and secure.

Suppliers would know that they could supply goods in confidence and know that they would get paid.

- **Corporate Social Responsibility**

  Most large businesses have a CSR report these days which explains how they are trying to do more than the minimum they need to do to comply with the law. There are many benefits to CSR[28] . Ryanair does not but if it had one this would help to show that it was taking its ethical responsibilities seriously.

Effect on stakeholders of improvements in this area

Shareholders and managers would be committed to identifying and making relevant improvements that would benefit the business.

Passengers and citizens would think more highly of the organisation.

Staff would be proud to work for the business.

Competitors would be under more pressure.

Benefit to the organisation of operating more ethically

Ryanair is a very successful airline which wants to continue expanding, but it is operating in a very competitive market. People know their rights these days and expect businesses they support to value them. If Ryanair wants to expand it has to be aware that now that it is an established, profitable company there is less excuse for acting as it did when it was a fledgling business desperate to make a profit. Now this sort of behaviour often just makes it look greedy and Michael O'Leary sometimes seems unprofessional.

By adopting more ethical policies and publicising these, it could attract more passengers which, overall, would help it to increase its profits. It would also be less vulnerable to unexpected problems or downturns in the travel business. I believe there is scope for improvements in all the areas I have identified without significantly increasing costs.

Adam Bell

10 May 2007

Reference sources

[1] Ryanair: Europe's Greenest Airline – Ryanair website (document dated September 2006) also Environmental Issues and Ryanair at www.ryanair.com/site/news/releases/2004/dec/gen-en-201204-3.html

[2] *Guardian* newspaper: Rise of low-cost flights comes at high price (5 January 2007)

[3] *Guardian* newspaper: Ryanair profits soar but O'Leary hits at Brown's tax (6 February 2007)

[4] *Mail on Sunday*: Jets do not cause wars and plague (17 January 2007) reproduced on www.thisismoney.co.uk/consumer/caring/article.html

5   BBC News: Virgin Atlantic move to save fuel (3 December 2006) at news.bbc.co.uk/1/hi/business/6203636.stm

6   Ryanair advert in Guardian in March 2007, reproduced on Indymedia Ireland at www.indymedia.ie/article/81705

7   Ryanair website – Mission statement and strategy document at www.ryanair.com

8   Ryanair website – Code of Business Conduct and Ethics and Ryanair's Passenger Service and Lowest Fares Charter

9   Ryanair reviews at travel.ciao.co.uk/reviews/ryanair

10 Ryanair passenger problems about Ryanair product and Ryanair service standards at www.airlinequality.com/forum/ryan.htm

11 *The Times*: Check-in charges help Ryanair fly higher (6 February 2007)

12 *Which* magazine consumer news: Fees weigh you down (May 2007)

13 *The Times*: O'Leary shows that less is more in air travel by James Harding, business editor (6 February 2007)

14 *Times Online*: How budget airlines boost profits with costly extras (7 April 2007) at www.timesonline.co.uk/tol/news/uk/article1624065.ece

15 Wikipedia at http://en.wikipedia.org/wiki/Ryanair

16 Ibid

17 Ryan Be Fair at www.ryan-be-fair.org

18 Management Issues – Ryanair staff bite back (11 January 2005) at www.management-issues.com/2006/5/25/blog/ryanair-staff-bite-back.asp

19 Ibid

20 Wikipedia at http:en.wikipedia.org/wiki/Ryanair

21 ASA Adjudication Ryanair Ltd at www.asa.org.uk/asa/adjudications/Public/TF_ADJ_41929.htm

22 Disability Rights Commission: Ryanair's policy on disabled customers – an update (21 October 2005) at http://www.drc-gb.org/newsroom/news_releases/2005/ryanairs_policy_on_disabled.aspx

23 Wikipedia at en.wikipedia.org/wiki/Ryanair

24 EDM1357 Ryanair's Treatment of Disabled Customers (25 April 2007) at http://edmi.parliament.uk/EDMi/EDMDetails.aspx?EDMID=33134&SESSION=885

25 Ryanair website at www.ryanair.com/site/about/invest/docs/2006/060901annualreport.pdf -

26 Corporate Governance Proxy Voting Activity September – November 2003 at www.westmids-pensions.org.uk/pdfs/corpgovactivityseptember03november03.pdf -

27 *Irish Times* Ryanair Investors question 1.48 billion offer (6 October 2006) at http://www.ireland.com/newspaper/finance/2006/1006/1158591432871.html

28 Corporate social responsibility at www.businesslink.gov.uk/bdotg/action/layer?topicId=1075408468

141

ASSESSOR FEEDBACK FORM

Learner Name: Adam Bell

Assignment ref 38.1, Task 4 (D1)

I really enjoyed reading your report, Adam, and found it very informative as it built upon the work you did for P1, P2 and M1.

I particularly liked your Introduction, which clearly and concisely summarised what you were writing about, and the fact that you dealt with each item in your second section separately, in bullet points with clear headings. This made your report easy to read. I was also impressed that you focused on specific areas on which you feel there is scope for improvement and gave evidence to support your arguments in each case. This is always far more effective than trying to include too much.

I was also impressed with your research. You have obviously used a wide range of sources and identified each of these at the end as requested. I was particularly pleased to find that you had cross-checked some of the claims on the Wikipedia website. As you know, because anyone can contribute to this site it may not always be totally accurate.

You have evaluated your ideas by looking at different stakeholder groups and also at the actions of competitors in many cases. Your conclusions were very appropriate and well-considered, particularly in the light of Ryanair's business model of keeping costs to a minimum and its expansion aims.

You have certainly achieved D1 with your report. Well done!